The Persistence of Religion

Harvey G. Cox is Hollis Professor of Divinity at Harvard University. One of the most famous theologians in America and beyond, his many influential books include *The Secular City* (1965), which became an international bestseller, *Many Mansions: A Christian's Encounter with Other Faiths* (1988), *When Jesus Came to Harvard: Making Moral Decisions Today* (2004) and *The Future of Faith* (2009). His research and teaching interests focus primarily on the interaction of religion, culture and politics. Among the issues he explores in his work are urbanization, theological developments in world Christianity, Jewish–Christian relations and spiritual movements – especially Pentecostalism – in a global setting.

Daisaku Ikeda is President of Soka Gakkai International, a Buddhist organization with some twelve million adherents in 192 countries and regions throughout the world. He is the author of over eighty books on Buddhist themes and received the United Nations Peace Award in 1983. His work to restore Chinese–Japanese relations as well as his contributions to world peace, cultural exchange and education have been widely recognized. The world's academic community has awarded him more than 250 academic degrees.

The Persistence of Religion

Comparative Perspectives on Modern Spirituality

Harvey Cox and
Daisaku Ikeda

I.B. TAURIS

LONDON · NEW YORK

Published in 2009 by I.B.Tauris & Co Ltd
6 Salem Road, London W2 4BU
175 Fifth Avenue, New York NY 10010
www.ibtauris.com

Distributed in the United States and Canada
Exclusively by Palgrave Macmillan
175 Fifth Avenue, New York NY 10010

Appendix 2 is published by permission of the Transnational Foundation for Peace
and Future Research, Sweden

ISBN (HB) 978 1 84885 194 8
ISBN (PB) 978 1 84885 195 5

A full CIP record for this book is available from the British Library
A full CIP record is available from the Library of Congress

Library of Congress Catalog Card Number: available

Typeset by JCS Publishing Services Ltd, www.jcs-publishing.co.uk
Printed and bound in Great Britain by CPI Antony Rowe, Chippenham

FSC
Mixed Sources
Product group from well-managed
forests and other controlled sources
Cert no. SGS-COC-2953
www.fsc.org
© 1996 Forest Stewardship Council

Contents

Preface by Harvey Cox

Why does religion persist in a modern or even postmodern age? Why does faith endure despite a recent spate of books advocating atheism? Why do I, as a Christian scholar who has spent so much of my career studying secularization, find myself involved in a dialogue with a distinguished Buddhist thinker such as Daisaku Ikeda?

My answer is that this book represents only a small part of what our present age demands. We need more than a dialogue between religions. We require a multifaceted conversation between world views, and this includes philosophies, ideologies and also secularism, atheism and agnosticism. In fact I am convinced that the crises the human race faces today can be addressed successfully only if we pool all our resources, and this can only happen if we learn to learn from each other. Such a willingness to learn in turn demands a measure of humility on everyone's part – a willingness to listen, and the frank recognition that *we could be mistaken*. In other words, I believe that an element of *uncertainty* is an indispensable ingredient in any mature faith. This includes atheists as well as religious people. I know and converse with atheists a fair amount, but the only ones I do not enjoy talking with are those who harbour no doubts about their atheism, the ones who seem absolutely sure they are right. They are, in effect, 'fundamentalist atheists'.

What is the connection between dialogue with Buddhists and dialogue with atheists? In my experience, Buddhists are usually not as preoccupied with atheism as Christians are. One can be a Buddhist with or without a traditional belief in God. But Christianity is different in this respect. The reality of God is quite central, therefore atheism is more of a challenge and more of a temptation. Further, any 'a-theism' is always a denial of some particular idea of God/god. Atheism, as my great teacher Paul Tillich (1886–1965) wrote, is always the shadow of some form of theism. Show me what God you do not believe in and maybe we will discover that I do not believe in that 'god' either.

Still, I believe that for any Christian, a certain kind of atheism must always be a temptation. This is probably true for other religious people as well. We should always remember that the atheists might be right, and we know this even in our own experience. Atheism announces itself in different ways. For me this 'atheist temptation' arrives with overtones of the famous words of Blaise Pascal, who confessed that when he thought about the farthest reaches of space and time, '. . . the eternal silence of these infinite spaces terrifies me.'

I began having these thoughts and fears when I was quite young, as soon as I learned that our solar system is only one infinitesimal speck in cosmos so immense it exceeds the range of normal numbers. It deepened when I learned that one day our planet would be burned to cinders by an exploding sun, which in turn would eventually disappear, along with all the memories and monuments of human life. There would remain only one vast, silent, empty void, with no one there even to observe it. Why would any God, I asked myself, concern himself with anything so minute and so transient? Who, quite honestly, has not felt a moment of Pascal's terror in the presence of such ideas?

But those vast empty spaces do not provide an answer. They pose a question. They can bespeak either terror or fascination, or probably both. I am convinced that a mature religious faith is one that keeps questions open, against all attempts at premature foreclosure. If an element of doubt is always an ingredient of faith, as I think it is, then I accept it. In one of his most eloquent passages, St Paul writes: 'Now hope that is seen is not hope. For who hopes for what he sees? But if we hope for what we do not see, we wait for it with patience' (Romans 8: 24, 25).

It may sound paradoxical, but it is by allowing, even welcoming, an element of this 'not seeing', of radical uncertainty, into my life, that I can face the terror Pascal spoke of without retreating either to a comforting religiosity that tries to expunge all uncertainty, or to a self-confident atheism that pretends to possess sure and certain answers it cannot possibly have. As I cultivate this religious 'uncertainty principle', I find that my conversations with Buddhists, including President Ikeda, have been especially nurturing. These honest exchanges continually remind me not only that my world view is one among many, but – more importantly – that this multidimensional way of living is spiritually more adult than is striving for some final resolution of the great mysteries of life. Therefore I do not consider Buddhists, or the followers of other religious paths, or open-minded atheists to be rivals or opponents. They are fellow travellers, and I welcome them, as I hope they welcome me.

As readers dip into this fascinating conversation between President Ikeda and me, it may be important to point out that I believe Christianity is not just a 'religion'. This is why I am still fascinated by those theologians, such as Dietrich Bonhoeffer, who asked us to imagine what form the message of Jesus might assume if, in the long course of evolution, 'religion' as we now define it somehow disappeared. Could there be such a thing as what Bonhoeffer called 'a non-religious interpretation of the Gospel'? Is it possible that religion, as he also once wrote, might be the 'outer garb' of the truth Jesus taught and demonstrated?

We now live in a time of what some see as 'resurgent' religion. Secularization appears to be in decline; therefore Bonhoeffer's query strikes us as somewhat irrelevant. Still, I have never been able to let go of his question. I am convinced that when Jesus spoke about the Kingdom of God, he had something far more comprehensive than some 'religious' alternative in mind. When he taught his disciples to pray that this Kingdom should come 'on earth as it is in heaven', he was referring to what Jews had called the *malkuth Yahweh*, the coming era of peace and plenty that includes the full sweep of liberated human living. He meant a utopia infinitely more far-reaching than any of the ones that the 'utopian' writers such as Thomas Campanella or Thomas More have tried to describe. Consequently, President Ikeda's emphasis on 'Buddhist humanism' evokes a positive response from me.

The Bible itself even hints at this reality-beyond-religion. There is no word for 'religion' in Old Testament Hebrew. In the New Testament, the book of Revelation describes the heavenly city, which is to appear on earth, as one in which '. . . there is no temple,' presumably because the Spirit of God pervades everything so that no separate 'spiritual' or 'religious' sphere is required.

I appreciate this insight because it means that in some important sense one does not have to be 'religious' in order to be a Christian, or to be a follower or friend of Jesus. It also coheres well with my conviction that the words 'belief' and 'believer' are ultimately of limited usefulness in matters of faith. I have already said above that I think there must always be a place for an element of doubt and uncertainty in faith. Otherwise it is not faith. And I know just too many 'non-believers' who have told me they often have doubts about their non-belief.

As a Christian I believe that we need the dialogue of world views because we are entering a new stage in Christian history, one in which 'faith' as a way of life is becoming more important than 'belief'. Belief is not the same as faith. Belief hovers near the upper, cognitive stratum of the self. It can come and go. It can be strong one day, weak the next. But faith locates itself in a deeper dimension. It is a matter of fundamental life orientation. The early Christians spoke of their faith as the 'way'. But in its journey through the Graeco-Roman cultural landscape, Christianity became increasingly identified with a set of beliefs that were then organized into creeds. Still, it did not have to happen that way.

I have come to the conviction that Christianity has emphasized 'belief' entirely too much, and is now transmuting itself into a stage that is 'beyond belief'. My new book, *The Future of Faith*, explores this tidal change.

It is here that the newly emerging conversation among the traditions may benefit mine the most. If historically Christianity has over-emphasized 'belief', it is a genuine strength of Buddhism that it has not. But this does not mean that we as Christians should merely discard our creeds. Rather, in future years we should understand them in a better way. We should appreciate them not as fences to separate us from other people, but as valiant attempts on the part of some Christians at certain specific moments in history to rethink their faith in the light of radically new cultural environments. However, we too now find ourselves in yet another new environment. We are entering an age of unprecedented religious and cultural diversity and a global world torn by hunger, injustice and the awful threat of nuclear catastrophe. But it is also a world bursting with fresh promise and new possibilities. It needs the collective wisdom that all our traditions bring to the table. This book represents one small contribution to that effort. I cannot conceive of an epoch in which I would prefer to have lived.

Harvey Cox

Preface by Daisaku Ikeda

Albert Camus (1913–60), an author I have been familiar with since my youth, wrote in unforgettable terms, 'To understand the world, a human being must reduce it to humanity and stamp a human mark on it.' How much do we actually understand about the world? To what extent are we aware of others' existence? How much do we care about the people who share the Earth with us?

For many centuries various ethnic groups, nations and religions have compiled their own versions of history. In many instances, the version seems to assume that the group to which it belongs is all important. Such histories ignore or marginalize everyone else. If they mention others at all, it is only with prejudice, contempt or extreme animosity. Ironically, in spite of the elimination of most geographical barriers by means of today's highly developed communication and transportation systems, the tendency to think in this way persists even in the twenty-first century. Indeed, the spread of the many distortions that accompany economic globalization makes people turn mentally still further inward. Professor Harvey G. Cox, an astute and keenly perceptive thinker and a leading scholar of religion, warns us most urgently about this situation. I am in complete agreement with him when he says that the historical protective device of demonizing everything strange and unknown has crippled mutual exchange and understanding. What came into being as self-protection can be used as a weapon to threaten the lives and lifestyles of other peoples. In the twentieth century, colonial oppression and forced assimilation, the pitiless racial segregation of apartheid and genocide such as the Holocaust – under the detestable term of the Final Solution – showed the extremes to which this attitude can lead. Anyone who raised a voice in protest against it was branded heretical or unpatriotic. But such so-called heretics are just the kind of people for whom Professor Cox has the greatest affection and respect: for instance, Mahatma Gandhi, the champion of Indian independence, killed by an assassin's bullet, and the great leader of the civil rights movement in the United States, Martin Luther King, Jr., Professor Cox's friend and companion.

As he explains in this book, Professor Cox was imprisoned for participating in King's peaceful demonstrations. This calls to mind the imprisonment of first Soka Gakkai president, Tsunesaburo Makiguchi (1871–1944), and his disciple and our second president, Josei Toda (1900–58), for opposing the policies of the Japanese militarist fascists during the Second World War. The experience gravely undermined Toda's health; Makiguchi died in prison at the advanced age of seventy-three. Neither of them ever wavered in his convictions. Their struggle was the glorious starting point of Soka Gakkai and Soka Gakkai International's (SGI) fervent quest for world peace.

I follow the path they pioneered. In 1974 and 1975, when the Cold War had split the world into East and West blocs and when the rift between China and the Soviet Union was widening, I visited both of those countries as well as the United States. As a citizen, for the sake of breaking down ideological barriers and building bridges of dialogue, I frankly discussed tension-reducing measures with Chinese premier Zhou Enlai, the Soviet leader Alexei N. Kosygin, and American secretary of state, Henry Kissinger. In the subsequent years, I have travelled to other countries, including Socialist states and countries in the former Communist bloc, to pave the way for cultural and educational exchanges intended to increase mutual understanding.

The persistent efforts by many people intensified the global desire for an end to the Cold War. As drops of water erode a boulder, twenty years ago, the people's patient efforts finally caused the apparently impregnable Cold War structure to crumble. The passing of the crisis, however, did not terminate conflict and internal strife, which still worsen among ethnic groups and religions, once again blanketing the Earth in chaotic darkness. It is a Sisyphean cycle, as in the myth that intrigued Camus. All his life Camus was fascinated by the Greek legend of Sisyphus, condemned forever to roll a boulder up a hill only to have it roll down again as soon as it reached the top.

I first met Professor Cox when the world began confronting this chaos. In September 1991, I was invited by the John F. Kennedy School of Government at Harvard to speak on the topic 'The Age of Soft Power and Inner Motivated Philosophy'. Among the many learned people assembled for the occasion, Professor Cox spoke to me in a voice of especially warm empathy. The following May, amidst the dazzling greenery of the Soka University Tokyo campus, we had a chance to talk more intimately; our topics naturally shifted to the issues surrounding the post-Cold War world and the role religion should play in dealing with them. Since the topic was too big to cover in a short time, at the conclusion of our conversations Professor Cox gave me what might be called a homework assignment: prepare to deliver another address at Harvard. After considerable serious thought, I was ready for a speech entitled 'Mahayana Buddhism and Twenty-First-Century Civilization', which I delivered in September 1993.

During our talks together, Professor Cox expressed his hope that Buddhism might serve as a bridge linking Christianity and Islam, to solve the long-standing problem between them. In line with this idea, I based my second Harvard speech on the idea of religion for the sake of humanity. 'In an age marked by widespread religious revival, we need always to ask: Does religion make people stronger or weaker? Does it encourage what is good or what is evil in them? Are they made better and wiser by religion?'

One week after this speech, SGI opened the Boston Research Center for the 21st Century (renamed the Ikeda Center for Peace, Learning, and Dialogue in July 2009), adjacent to the Harvard campus, to serve as a headquarters for promoting intercultural and inter-religious dialogues to overcome the issues confronting humanity. As founder, I would like to take this chance to offer wholehearted thanks to Professor Cox and the many others who have cooperated with and supported the centre's work. We are all extremely grateful.

This dialogue is the fruit of many years of correspondence and exchange between Professor Cox and me. The role of religion in building a global society of peace and symbiosis has interested us both from the very outset. The book contains our thoughts on this question. In addition, it ranges over a wide field of other topics, including non-violence – with reference to the history of Martin Luther King's civil rights struggle – the evils of materialism, the pros and cons of the Internet society, the elimination of nuclear arms, and university education. I am delighted that this English-language version is following the Japanese edition. In connection with its publication, I want to offer warmest thanks to Iradj Bagherzade, chairman and publisher of I.B.Tauris & Co. Ltd, to the translator Richard L. Gage, and to all other parties involved.

As I recall vividly, during our dialogue, in connection with his caution against the current spread of fundamentalism, Professor Cox said, 'As long as I am asking the question, I remain fully human.' Religions and ethnic groups must not try to impose unilaterally on others the beliefs that they assume to be absolute. Instead, we must all continue questioning together.

We face the task of creating a world of respect for humanity in a peaceful society, transcending ethnic and religious differences. Our view – and the message we want this book to convey – is that the way to such a new world will open up only in a setting of open-minded mutual discussion. We hope this

English-language edition of our dialogue will take our message to a wider audience and provide food for thought and action, especially among young people, who bear the responsibility for future generations.

Daisaku Ikeda

ONE

Beyond the Clash of Civilizations

Ikeda: I am honoured to have a chance to engage in a dialogue with a religious scholar of your calibre, Professor Cox. You were a commentator when I delivered a speech at Harvard University in autumn 1993. That was one of the most treasured experiences of my life and I consider the friendship we have maintained since then most precious.

Cox: When you delivered that address, I was chairman of the Harvard Department of Applied Theology. I remember being delighted that you selected as your topic the meaning of humanity and life and death. Your speech was entitled 'Mahayana Buddhism and Twenty-First-Century Civilization'. Many Harvard scholars had hoped and anticipated that you would choose just such a subject.

Ikeda: It is very kind of you to say so. I remember that the late economist John Kenneth Galbraith attended the address. In conjunction with such other inextricably related themes as scientific advances and bioethics and human spiritual devastation, dealing with the issue of life and death is more significant now than

1

ever before. I hope that, taking peace and religion as our main thread, you and I will be able to discuss them and other matters confronting the modern world from many different angles. In addition, there are a number of perspectives set out in my Harvard speech that I want to pursue a little more deeply.

Cox: By all means, let's discuss them. We have a duty to address coming generations, for the sake of building a better, peaceful future.

Ikeda: It is still fresh in my mind that, in your comments at Harvard, you said that humanity is now approaching the end of the secular age. In the nineteenth century, Nietzsche proclaimed the death of God. Modern society has tended to reject religion as unscientific and as something that dwarfs human beings. But materialism and total reliance on the omnipotence of science have hollowed out the human spirit and created a barbarous world of conflict. It seems, however, that – as is witnessed by various Islamic movements and the vitalization of conservative Christian faith in the United States – the influence of religion is growing stronger, and awareness of religiosity in society is increasing.

Cox: Very true. In my commentary on your speech, I countered Nietzsche's proclamation by insisting that God is not dead yet. I welcome the revival of religion. But religion can become either medicine or poison. It can open people's fields of vision and help them see the whole picture. On the other hand, it can become narrow and very exclusivist. For this reason, dialogue is paramount.

Ikeda: I agree. I am delighted that we have the chance to engage in further dialogue on this topic. For many years you have demonstrated profound understanding of the Soka Gakkai International movement of culture, peace and education. I should like to take this opportunity to thank you once again for your support. Without open dialogue, religion can become self-righteous and self-engrossed. When that happens, religion runs the danger of being a source, not of happiness, but of conflict and misery. It is then not true religion. The same kind of thing applies in cultural, ethnic and national relations. Lack of dialogue generates friction and conflict and, in the opinion of some, can lead to what is called the 'clash of civilizations', a term that originated at Harvard.

The Time for Intercultural Dialogue is Now – Our Best Opportunity

Cox: Yes. To some extent, all of us at Harvard are aware of the shadow of Professor Samuel Huntington and his idea of the conflict of civilizations.

Ikeda: Ever since he published his seminal essay 'The Clash of Civilizations?' in the journal *Foreign Affairs* in 1993, public debate of his idea has raged. The shadow it cast over the minds of people indicates the gravity of the problems confronting our world today. It is undeniable that increasingly frequent and more violent ethnic and religious clashes in many regions make us all uneasy.

Cox: Yes, but I think we are not fated to have a conflict of civilizations at all. And I am especially concerned that Professor Huntington sees a religion at the core of the conflicts of the civilizations he examines. More than a mere mistake, to presume that a Judaeo-Christian religion, an Islamic religion, a Sinic religion, an Indic religion, and so on is the cause of conflict arouses unnecessary fear and apprehension among people.

Ikeda: I agree. Huntington's idea – which I have discussed with Majid Tehranian, the Iranian-born peace scholar – is that international conflicts will break out between different civilizations: the Christian, the Muslim, the Confucian and so on. But this approach ignores the various other causes of conflict. In addition, it breeds imaginary enemies, between whom mutual understanding becomes impossibility. The kind of prediction that Huntington makes can, itself, generate prejudice and a vicious circle of new conflicts.

Cox: That is so. In a speech at the United Nations a few years ago, Seyyed Mohammad Khatami, former president of Iran, said that we need, not a conflict of civilizations, but a dialogue of cultures. I like to think that the current moment is not one of inevitable conflict, but one in which we have the best opportunity we have ever had for true dialogue. We must create occasions and places for it and invite people to participate.

Ikeda: Indeed we must. Ours is a time when people of different cultures and languages come into contact, engage in exchanges and influence each other on a global scale with unprecedented speed. This is why the importance of dialogue steadily increases. As Mr Khatami said, dialogue is the way to understand others and arrive at truths. Advocates of inter-civilization dialogues recognize the value of wisdom and make reason based on wisdom the foundation of life. Terrorism and bloody ethnic conflicts are less clashes of civilization than clashes of the anger, egoism and brutality inherent in life and disguised as narrow nationalism and fanatical religious ideas.

Cox: This conversation between you and me is one very small example of the kind of thing we need at all levels – not just among university professors and people of your status. We need these kinds of conversations everywhere.

Ikeda: Yes. And I hope our dialogue will contribute to making the twenty-first a century of intercultural and inter-civilization dialogue.

Understanding Our Shared Ardour and Compassion

Cox: Immigration patterns, travel and other considerations enable people to meet in all kinds of ways. Some of the best conversations and cultural exchanges take place, not in seminar rooms, but in places where people meet informally, as in coffee shops, in their own homes, at the workplace, in college laboratories, or travelling on the road.

Ikeda: The best dialogue requires informality and openness. Effective, lively and warm, mind-to-mind exchanges are of the utmost importance. We need to stress our shared humanity. We must realize that people of different races and cultural backgrounds have beloved family and friends, and that they experience the same joys and sorrows that we experience. Dialogue must embody the fervour and compassion we all share as human beings.

Cox: Many human beings, at least at first encounter, tend to be suspicious or apprehensive of someone who appears to be different. They look different and have a different culture, a different language, a different religion and different economic patterns. Perhaps because of evolutionary biology, first reactions tend to be cautious and prompt us to ask, 'Who are these people?'

Ikeda: Very true. Even people who intellectually realize the equality of all humans tend to be made uneasy by encounters with people who are different.

Cox: Such uneasiness can easily turn into xenophobia, which we must strive against. We can't just say this is a bad thing and shouldn't happen. Instead of merely hoping intercultural or cross-cultural dialogue will take place, we must provide occasions for them.

Ikeda: And we must find ways to practise dialogue in society itself.

Cox: Yes. I am very grateful to you for this opportunity to engage in dialogue. You have conducted similar dialogues with almost innumerable thoughtful people and have published them for the world to read. With your encouragement, this kind of dialogue and exchange is actively promoted and occupies a central position at Soka University, just as it does at Harvard. I believe one of the major purposes of a university is to encourage dialogue. I am glad to make a small contribution in the form of this exchange with you.

Ikeda: I am grateful for your encouraging words. During my discussions with him over thirty years ago, the British historian Arnold J. Toynbee told me that dialogue is the only way to open the way for humanity and urged me – I was young at the time – to carry on the work of discussing important things with intellectuals from all over the world. I promised to do so and have kept my promise to the best of my ability.

You are a world-famous theologian. I am a Buddhist. Our religious and cultural backgrounds differ; we were born and raised in different countries. But both of us strive for the peace and happiness of humanity. It is my sincere wish that our conversation may make a contribution to improving the prospects of humanity.

Cox: I share that wish.

The Upheaval of the Second World War – Hard Times for the Young

Ikeda: We are nearly the same age: you were born in 1929 and I in 1928. Where were you born?

Cox: In the small country town of Malvern, Pennsylvania, on the edge of a purely rural area. We had forests and meadows and horses all within close walking distance. Philadelphia was only twenty-two miles away, but when I was a small boy that was a greater distance than it is now. I grew up with a deep appreciation for nature. I understand you spent your young years on the seashore.

Ikeda: Deeply engraved in my memory, those were days of formative encounters with nature. I was born and raised in a place called Ota, on the shore of Tokyo Bay. In those days it was a lovely natural place; the sea was still clean.

Cox: Speaking of the natural environment reminds me of *Rendezvous with Nature,* your published collection of photographs of nature over the four seasons of the year. I enjoy your photographs: you know how to convey the elegance of flowers and trees in a way that reveals your love of nature.

Ikeda: Thank you for saying so. I am not a professional; a friend once gave me a camera in the hope that photography would be a way for me to relax. I simply try to capture on film the natural scenes I encounter during my leisure hours or from the window of the car or the train when I am travelling during my work. At the strong request of our members, my photographs are on display in various localities in our buildings.

Paintings are perhaps less accessible, but, framed and displayed on a wall, photographs of beautiful flowers and greenery become windows that open on the world, enabling us to enjoy the beauties of nature even while we live in big cities. They can convey a sense of fresh air as well as of light.

But to return to your early family life, what was your father like?

Cox: My father ran a small house-decorating business. He didn't do much of the actual work himself but negotiated contracts,

7

hired painters and paper-hangers, and tried to collect the money. For a while he even ran a store selling household-improvement goods.

Ikeda: My family ran a business preparing and selling edible seaweeds. At one time it prospered enough to hire a large number of workers. But later, with the great Kanto earthquake of 1923, my father's poor health and the conscription of my four brothers who had worked for him, the business declined. The family found it hard to make ends meet.

Cox: Like yours, my childhood coincided with the tumult of the Great Depression and of the Second World War. During the war, when many others were prospering, my father's business fell on hard times because, instead of being put to civilian uses, all the paint was being used for ships and tanks, and because workers were all being drafted. As his business went downhill, my father experienced a dreadful crisis. He felt extremely bad about no longer being able to support his family adequately. It really undermined his self-esteem.

Ikeda: War brought unhappiness to tens of millions of families. Seeing four of his sons called up for military service was a tremendous blow to my father. The oldest was killed in Burma at the age of twenty-nine. I shall never forget my mother's look of pain upon receiving notification of his death.

Cox: I can sympathize with your parents.

When the family business failed, my own father went to work at Wyeth Laboratories, a large operation that eventually produced penicillin. His duties were similar to what he had done when he ran his own business: managing the transportation division, making sure products were properly received and dispatched, and hiring and firing truck drivers and supervisors. He was good at the work and was appreciated as a good boss. In my late teens, I too worked at Wyeth during the summer as a low-level assistant truck driver, loading, unloading and fuelling trucks. Doing this kind of work was good experience.

Ikeda: Yes, it must have been. For a while in my boyhood I delivered newspapers, and the experience of that work has stood me in good stead to this day. As the war intensified, I went to work in a steel plant producing munitions. My work there with metal processing and operating a lathe was by no means wasted experience. But life was punishing for me in the dark days of militarism. For one thing, the food shortage was painful. Furthermore I suffered from lung disease.

Cox: That must have been very hard on you.

On the basis of my own life, I have come to believe that children should have work experience. It teaches them responsibility and about turning their hands to something and achieving goals. If they do their work well, they earn praise. If not, they are criticized.

Ikeda: Yes. Over a century ago, Tsunesaburo Makiguchi, educator and first president of Soka Gakkai, advocated a school system whereby children did classroom work for half the day and practical work for the other half. His system taught them vital things about life.

Recollections of Fathers – Deep Compassion and Rage against War

Cox: That is important. One of my first responsibilities on the job at Wyeth was to back a truck through a garage door. Although I tried to be careful, I scraped the side of the vehicle. The other drivers treated me to a lot of ridicule; I felt terrible. But when I told my father I wanted to quit the job, he said, 'C'mon, you think you are the first person who ever scraped the side of a truck? Of course not. You'll do better next time.' He was right.

Ikeda: Your father sounds a wonderful man. Though apparently simple, his words shine with a deep philosophy of life. Mistakes are nothing to be afraid of. As is famous in history, the great inventor Thomas Edison made an immense number of mistakes before finally succeeding in inventing the incandescent light bulb.

Cox: When the time came, my father was glad to send me to college. No doubt, if he had still been running his own business, inherited from his father, he would have wanted me or my brother to take it over. But the business was gone after the war, and he was working for a larger firm.

I went to the University of Pennsylvania, where I became interested in philosophy, ethics, international relations, religion and so on. Later I went on to Harvard and my lifelong teaching in the field of religion.

Ikeda: Your father seems to have understood you better than anyone else.

Cox: Yes. From him I learned about parenting in a way that combines gentle supervision, advice and counsel with instruction in right and wrong and a great deal of freedom. For example, when I was seventeen, before graduating from high school, I told my father I wanted to join the merchant marines. He replied, 'If that's what you want to do, then do it.' (I doubt I would have allowed my own son to take such a step at seventeen.) Father was demonstrating his belief that I had reached the age to make responsible decisions. I did what I wanted.

Ikeda: When you were seventeen, the Second World War had just ended. Travel abroad was difficult then, even for United States citizens. I imagine your father was very worried about you.

Cox: Thinking back now, I can see that he made a very permissive decision. He did not say, 'What? You are only seventeen!' But he allowed me to do it, and it was a great experience. For two successive years, during the summers only, I travelled to and from Europe on merchant ships.

Ikeda: That must have been a great journey for a young man. In thinking about my own father, I recall how, during the war, I secretly volunteered for the Youth Air Corps. Under the influence of the prevailing militaristic education, I naively wanted to serve my homeland. The times were like that. But when a military representative turned up at our house, my father angrily chased him away. 'Three of my sons are already in the military, and the fourth's about to go. Now you want to take the fifth boy away! That's too much!' Then he gave me the worst scolding I'd ever had. He was usually taciturn, but on this occasion I caught a glimpse of his strong determination not to sacrifice any more of his sons.

Cox: Your father's anger against the war reveals the depth of his love for his family.

Parental Heritage – The Spirit of Hope and Peace

Ikeda: What was your mother like?

Cox: My mother was very organized, warm and personable. She never worked outside the home but concentrated on running the household. And that was plenty because I had three siblings. Some of my mother's brothers and sisters and their children lived in our town, so our house was always full of cousins and uncles who relied on my mother's efficient organization. She was very direct in her speech, never reluctant to say things that seemed blunt, but did so in a tone that was never condemnatory.

Ikeda: I can tell how you felt about her in the way that you describe her behaviour.

My own mother was a very strong person. Let me share one vivid memory. In 1945, the last year of the war, the house we had just moved into suffered a direct hit by an incendiary bomb during an air raid. A set of Girl's Day dolls was practically all that remained of our family's household goods. Later, as we stood dumbfounded among the ruins, mother briskly said, 'I just know we're going to move into another house where we can display these dolls.' Her words inspired us all with hope.

Cox: Your story is very touching. It hints at the wrath you feel for war. As a protestor against the Vietnam War, that anger resonates strongly with my own sentiments.

My father came from an old tradition of Quakers. Though not a Quaker himself, because of this background, he was always suspicious of violence. My mother came from Methodists influenced by the anti-military mentality of the Mennonites. So, on both sides I inherited a distrust of the military.

Ikeda: The Quakers are thoroughgoing pacifists and advocates of non-violence, as I learned from Dr Elise Boulding, a Quaker with whom I shared a dialogue.

Philadelphia, the capital of your state, was founded by the Quaker William Penn, on ideals of peace and religious freedom. I know that the Methodists, who were firm Abolitionists, take a great interest in social problems and support educational equality.

Cox: Yes, those attitudes were part of my background. My parents were not at all fond of the military. Sometimes they were very disparaging of it, even to the point of ridicule. They thought dressing up in uniform and marching around beating drums was silly and pretentious.

Not particularly pious or churchgoing, they were both wary of established religion, too. They believed in Christian ethics; sometimes they would attend church and sometimes not. They were suspicious of hierarchy, of people who made money out of the Church, and of excessively strict, narrow religious views. They thought we should be broad-minded and tolerant.

The Challenge of Realizing Ideals Received from Mentors

Ikeda: I see your parents were very sensible people with strong wills. Who among your teachers is most vivid in your memory?

Cox: When I came to Harvard, my main mentor was the late James Luther Adams. He was a wonderfully supportive, helpful, attentive and concerned mentor. He was my major source of mentorship. Then I studied with Paul Tillich. I admired him and learned much from him, but I didn't consider him a mentor. He was an intellectual stimulus and in some ways both a critic and a supporter.

Ikeda: At the age of nineteen, I met Josei Toda and became a member of Soka Gakkai. Mr Toda and his mentor Mr Makiguchi were both incarcerated for resisting the militarists during the Second World War. Mr Makiguchi died in prison but Mr Toda survived to struggle alone to rebuild Soka Gakkai in post-war Japan. He was my tutor in Buddhism, of course, but also in many fields of learning. He helped me plan for the future.

Cox: Yes, I know.

Ikeda: He also instructed me to participate in dialogues with intellectuals from all over the world and to seek ways to achieve peace. From the 1950s, he advocated global citizenship. The idea that humanity is one race fated to live in one great community was virtually unknown in the Japan of those days. The Toda Institute for Global Peace and Policy Research, which I founded, deals enthusiastically with inter-civilization dialogues with the aim of realizing Mr Toda's ideals. This dialogue with you is part of my answer to the challenge of that undertaking. In the next chapter I hope to discuss non-violence and your encounter with Martin Luther King, Jr., who exerted a great influence on your philosophy and life.

TWO

Martin Luther King, Jr. and the Spirit of Non-Violence

_____

Ikeda: There is no undertaking as serious as a life dedicated to the struggle of faith and shared with comrades in truth. The history of the great battle for justice and human rights is immortal. In it, you and Martin Luther King, Jr., leader of the civil rights movement in the United States, fulfilled a supreme mission. As you told me when we discussed the matter once in Tokyo, both you and he were born in 1929. I understand that you first met in 1956.

Cox: Yes. It was just after he had started the bus boycott in Montgomery, Alabama.

Ikeda: Where did that first meeting take place?

Cox: In Nashville, Tennessee. I was taking summer courses in theology and German at Vanderbilt University. I chose a southern university because I was especially committed to working on racial justice. While at Vanderbilt, I went to hear Dr

King speak. He was already becoming well known, though not nearly as well known as he was later.

Ikeda: This was at a time when, under his leadership, the American civil rights movement was swelling and expanding. Some wonderful connection must have brought you together in response to that historic moment.

Cox: When we met in person we discovered we had several things in common. Born the same year, we both studied to be Baptist ministers. We both had similar intellectual interests. For example, we were both interested in the work of the German-American theologian Paul Tillich.

Ikeda: You studied with Tillich, as you mentioned earlier. I can easily see how you and Dr King felt deep, mutual, intellectual and spiritual sympathy as friends and fellow champions of human rights.

Cox: Yes. At about this time Martin Luther King, Jr. said to me, 'I really want to be a theology and religion professor, but my father has told me that first I ought to be a pastor at a local church and learn from the ground up. So I went back to Montgomery to be a minister at a black Baptist church there. But at some time I really want to devote my life to being a theology professor.' He never got a chance to do that.

Ikeda: In his stead, you went on to study and to make achievements of worldwide significance in the fields of theology and religious studies. I am sure that the work of his great and close friend would have delighted Dr King.

Cox: Thank you for saying so.

Participation in the Civil Rights Movement – Unjust Arrest and Imprisonment

Ikeda: What prompted you to participate in the civil rights struggle?

Cox: Malvern, Pennsylvania, the little town where I grew up, had a small group of African-American inhabitants. All of us children – black and white – attended the same school. The town was too small to have segregated schools. So back in the 1930s, in an already racially integrated school, I got to know and make friends with my black classmates. As I grew older, I noticed that they were discriminated against in employment, education and various other areas. I knew this was wrong. We were all created equal and should all have equal opportunities. Some of my black classmates were just as bright as, or even brighter than, the whites but still faced a racial barrier. At college I became even more convinced that the situation was wrong and gradually came to want to do something about it. I hoped to make work for racial reconciliation one of the main parts of my teaching and my ministry.

Ikeda: Your purpose was noble. Although, as they grow older, people often lose their youthful purity of mind, you persisted in the aspirations that guided you from your young days and boldly spoke out against social evil and discrimination. I have the greatest respect for the strong belief that enabled you to do this. Both your participation in the civil rights struggle and your scholarly work in the field of religious studies are a continuation of that same persistence.

I understand that your friendship with Dr King remained unchanged.

Cox: Our friendship lasted over the years until he was killed in 1968. I saw him frequently. I attended meetings of the Southern Christian Leadership Conference (SCLC) and once, when they

17

met in Birmingham, Alabama, he invited me to give the keynote address. That was a great moment in my life. We marched together. We consulted. I invited him to visit Oberlin College, in Oberlin, Ohio, when I was chaplain there. Then later, he came to Harvard a couple of times when I started teaching there.

Ikeda: You and he shared a history of profound exchanges. During your participation in the civil rights movement, you, too, were unjustly arrested and imprisoned, I believe.

Cox: Yes. I was one of a group of demonstrators who'd been protesting the racial injustice of depriving African Americans of the right to vote and access to restaurants. After a peaceful demonstration in North Carolina, we were arrested. But the jail became so full that I was moved to another one. Our principal worry was that we didn't know exactly what they were going to charge us with. People arrested during the civil rights movement were usually charged with misdemeanours such as demonstrating or parading without a permit. In our case, however, the authorities had obtained a superior court order to stop the parade because they argued we would incite violence, even though we were non-violent. We nonetheless went ahead with our plans, violating a superior court injunction at the state level and making ourselves liable to imprisonment for two to five years. I was terrified. Eventually those charges were dropped, and we got only a few days. We had to promise never to go to that town again.

Ikeda: I honour the courage with which, careless of your own personal danger, you fought bravely in the front lines of the struggle.

Only a person who has been imprisoned knows what it feels like. In 1957, I was jailed for about two weeks on trumped-up charges of violating election laws. Behind this was the manoeuvring of authorities that were fearful of the rise of Soka Gakkai as a new, popular force. I was subjected to severe interrogations and intimidated with threats of the imprisonment of my mentor, Josei Toda. Knowing that he was in a physically weakened condition, I felt that I must protect him at all costs.

The court battles dragged on for four and a half years. Finally I was exonerated, but the experience left me with a deep impression of the tyranny of authorities who despise and wish to suppress the masses.

Cox: That is understandable. I, too, have witnessed the fearsomeness of authority.

Later Martin Luther King, Jr. and I marched together in Selma, Alabama. I worked with him in St Augustine, Florida, and accompanied him to some of the rallies and talks he gave in various places. But the high point came at that meeting of the SCLC in 1966 in Birmingham. I will never forget when he introduced me and then, after my talk, thanked me. Those were unforgettable moments.

Persevering in Spite of Mortal Risk – The Heritage of the Spirit of Non-Violence

Ikeda: What you say reveals a clear picture of what those times were like. Not only African Americans, but also many white people respected and sympathized with Martin Luther King, Jr. You were one of his close associates. What about him appealed to you most?

Cox: I admired him for two main reasons. First, he was an unequivocal supporter of non-violence. He would say, 'I don't care if everyone else in the United States, every black, every white, everybody advocates violence, I will continue to advocate non-violence, because it is the only way to solve human problems without humiliating the other person. The other person, too, is a child of God and must not be harmed. You don't defeat your enemies, you win them over if possible, and non-violence is the way to do that.' He believed that with all his heart.

Ikeda: Leaders all over the world should memorize those words. Violence breeds more violence and intensifies hatred. Only the spirit of non-violence can sever the endless chain of violence. Acting on it, however, is not as easy as saying it. According to Gandhi, practising non-violence takes more courage than practising violence. Gandhi made this comment to Benjamin Elijah Mays – the sixth president of Morehouse College, Dr King's alma mater – who travelled to India to learn about non-violent struggle from Gandhi himself. Thus Gandhi's spirit of non-violence crossed the ocean with Mays, who passed it on to Martin Luther King, Jr., who made it the mainstay of the civil rights movement.

Cox: Without doubt, Jesus and Gandhi were the two major influences on King's life. In connection with Gandhi's words, you mentioned courage. The second thing that I appreciated about King was his absolute, sheer, physical courage – the courage to walk into screaming mobs of people who were throwing things and screaming insults, and calmly lead us with no sense of anger, and assure the rest of us that everything would be all right. Afterwards he would ask us, 'Did I look frightened?' We would always say, 'No, Dr King.'

You have to confront your own fear and hatred. If people insult you, throw things at you and try to harm you, never respond with either inward or outward hatred. You must respond with love. You have to love your enemy. Jesus said this, and King believed it. He knew it is hard to do but insisted that people who cannot do it should not be involved in the civil rights movement.

Ikeda: That is a valuable testimony. During the movement, many African Americans became victims. Extreme white seg-regationalists shot or beat them to death; black people's houses were bombed. Some black people argued that non-violence would solve nothing and that violence must be met with violence. But this cry never became general because, standing in the forefront, through his own actions, Martin Luther King, Jr. demonstrated the might of the human spirit. Gandhi once told Mays that exhortation will not temper people. Non-violence must be practised, not just preached. Martin Luther King, Jr. led the civil rights movement with his own practical actions.

Cox: As you know, towards the end of his life, King said that violence is the wrong way to deal not only with domestic issues such as racism, but also with international affairs. We cannot have a world in which we try to solve problems by wars. We have reached the end of the period in human history in which war can be an acceptable option. So, at the end of his life, he strongly opposed the Vietnam War and the build-up of American military power.

Ikeda: The greatest violence of which human beings are capable, war is unforgivable. At the time, at a gathering of young people and students, I called for the immediate cessation of the Vietnam War and sent President Nixon a letter to that effect. Martin Luther King, Jr. was assassinated in Memphis, Tennessee, in April 1968, two years after he publicly opposed the war in Vietnam. I cannot help thinking that, for a man who had abjured violence all his life, to be killed by an assassin's bullet only shows the deep-rootedness of the issues with which King struggled.

Cox: As is clear from papers and conversations that have recently come to light, in the last weeks of his life, King suspected that he would soon be killed. He struggled with the likelihood, not because he was afraid of death, but because he didn't want his wife to be widowed or his children left without a father. That was very hard for him. I have a feeling – and this is only a guess – that after he was shot, he thought, 'It has finally happened and I am following even unto death the same pattern as Jesus.' I think this was probably his understanding of what was happening to him.

Ikeda: You demonstrate the insight of a deeply devoted friend. Though he died far too soon – at the early age of thirty-nine – he left a shining mark on history. His life shed a bright, immortal light on human history and we must not permit the soul of his martyrdom to fade. As Dr Lawrence E. Carter, director of the King International Chapel at Morehouse College, has said, the important thing today is to pass on the spirit of non-violence for which King gave his life. But we must do more than merely pass it on. As King himself did, we must courageously live and work among the people. Only those who endure actual suffering and struggle their way to the goal can be rightfully called his heirs.

Cox: I agree. We must pass on to posterity the justice, liberty and equality that were his lifelong goals.

The Tragedies of the Kennedy Family, True Supporters of the Civil Rights Movement

Ikeda: John F. Kennedy was well known as a supporter of the civil rights movement. You were on the staff of his brother Robert Kennedy when he was campaigning for the presidential nomination.

To my sorrow, plans for me to meet President Kennedy were delayed until the opportunity was lost forever. In January 1978, when he visited Japan, Senator Edward Kennedy, the youngest of the brothers, called on me for a discussion. Please share some of your memories of the Kennedys.

Cox: I have especially vivid memories of Robert Kennedy. In 1968, the year in which King was killed, I worked very hard on his presidential nomination campaign. I took some time off from Harvard. At that point – five years after John Kennedy died – Bobby Kennedy became a strong critic of the Vietnam War and a vigorous advocate of racial and economic justice. These were the three pillars of his platform. He was a very attractive, energetic and eloquent candidate.

Ikeda: As is well known, Attorney General Robert Kennedy supported his brother's efforts in the civil rights movement.

On 4 April, the day of the King assassination, enraged African Americans all over the country rioted. Property was destroyed, and more than forty people lost their lives. In a brief speech he made at the time in Indianapolis, Indiana, Robert Kennedy said,

> We can move in that direction as a country, in great polarization – black people amongst black, white people amongst white, filled with hatred toward one another. Or we can make an effort, as Martin Luther King, Jr. did, to understand and to comprehend, and to replace that violence, that stain of bloodshed that has spread across our land, with an effort to understand with compassion and love.
>
> What we need in the United States is not division; what we need in the United States is not hatred; what we need in the United States is not violence or lawlessness, but love and wisdom, and compassion toward one another, and a feeling of justice toward those who still suffer within our country, whether they be white or they be black.

Before his speech, the police warned Robert Kennedy that they could not guarantee his safety and urged him not to appear before the crowd. But he overlooked the warning in the desire to express his feelings directly to as many people as possible. In contrast to the violence in many other cities, no rioting occurred in Indianapolis, where Kennedy spoke.

Cox: You have touched on an important historical fact. Bobby was a truly courageous person who always had warm regard for the poor and downtrodden. I accepted his request to be a part of his presidential nomination campaign and gave speeches, mainly to college students, in two or three states. I went from one college to another talking about him and actually was in Los Angeles, California, the day he was killed there.

Ikeda: On the day on which he won the California primary?

Cox: Yes, ironically. During that day, when we saw that things were going pretty well, I decided to fly back home to teach classes. I took a night flight from Los Angeles International to Boston, arriving the next morning, only to learn that Bobby had been shot. It was in June 1968, only two months after the assassination of Dr King.

Ikeda: He had just finished a victory speech before 2,000 campaign workers at the Ambassador Hotel in Los Angeles, when a young man approached him and suddenly fired his weapon.

Cox: When I first heard of the assassination, Bobby was not dead yet but was still lingering in the hospital. I was terribly upset; everything seemed to be lost. All the political developments I thought possible under him were gone, and I wanted to leave the United States, at least for a time. So I took my young family and moved for a couple of months to Cuernavaca, close to Mexico City. While there, I tried to piece together what was happening in America and to discover whether there was any hope left for a country that seemed bent on killing its best citizens – John Kennedy, Martin Luther King, Jr. and Bobby Kennedy. It was a perfectly dreadful, horrendous time.

A Life of Fortitude Confronting Despair and Hardship

Ikeda: I can imagine how you must have suffered at the loss, one after another, of your best friends. The whole world was shocked at the assassination of a series of great leaders in the land of liberty and democracy. While leading the free nations and lauding economic prosperity, the United States had grave

24

internal problems such as racial discrimination and poverty and was split over the quagmire of the Vietnam War. The series of tragic killings seemed to me to symbolize an America sinking in division and confusion.

What was your life in Mexico like?

Cox: I was almost a dropout. I had a job teaching at a small academy. Cuernavaca is a beautiful little city with a pleasant, warm climate. I could have stayed there. It was very tempting to distance myself from the whole calamity at home. But after serious conversations, my wife and I decided to return to the United States, where I became even more deeply involved in opposition to the Vietnam War.

Ikeda: You preserved your ideals even in the face of great hardships.

Cox: Yes, I did. I think friends and colleagues who did not give up prevented my giving up. I told myself we had to keep going. The situation looked – and was – terrible, but we had to continue struggling non-violently. We had to.

I have always thought that living a spiritual and moral and socially effective life is not something you do alone. It is not a solo flight. It has to be something done together with people who support you and encourage you, while you encourage and support them as well. Otherwise it becomes an enormously lonely and discouraging enterprise. In my case, I didn't become negative because I had such people around me.

Harvard was very kind. They gave me a leave of absence while I was going through all this but said I was welcome to return to teach if I wanted to. I did so and resumed teaching.

Ikeda: I agree with you entirely when you say that life is not a solo flight. My own mentor, Josei Toda, used the revolutionary novel *The Eternal City*, by Hall Caine (1853–1931), to teach young people the importance of bonds of friendship and comradeship.

The support and encouragement of friends with similar goals enable human beings to overcome hardships and achieve great things that they could not achieve alone.

In one of his plays, the German poet and playwright Friedrich Schiller (1759–1805) described friendship as sincere and bold and declared that one character is ready to do battle with the whole world side-by-side with his fearless friend. Sincere friendship is one of the greatest treasures of life. I am proud to have wonderful friends of many different philosophical and religious backgrounds all over the world. It is my cherished wish to be able to work with my friends, including you, to build a century of peace and respect for human rights.

THREE

The Market Economy and the Role of Religion

Cox: In a conversation we had when I visited Japan in 1992, you said young Japanese people today have everything they want. In comparison with the past, Japan is now very prosperous. Still, although they have the latest things, the Japanese are not happy.

Ikeda: Many people are concerned about this. In Japan today, as the economic gap widens, people tend to pursue material wealth with increasing avidity. But, obviously, it is a mistake to equate material property with the truly best way to live.

Cox: Yes it is. Today we are bombarded with messages about the things we need and how to acquire them. But we really do not need all those things; acquiring them conveys no spiritual satisfaction. A person with two cars is sure to want a third. If he has a television apiece in three rooms, he will want one for the fourth and fifth rooms as well. The yearning is always for a bigger colour television, a new computer, and so on.

Ikeda: You are right. Unbridled greed is characteristic of modern society. Developments in technology and the market economy thrust individual greed on the path of increasing hypertrophy. Human greed was the final topic of the dialogue I shared with the English historian Arnold J. Toynbee.

Cox: It is a very important theme. I discussed it once in an article called 'The Market as God'. There has always been a market in human history. The market has always played an important social role. But, in the last hundred years or so, it has become too influential – the dominant source of values and meanings in the consumer advertising culture. For instance, advertising constantly defines the good life, as if saying, 'If you don't have all these material possessions, there must be something wrong with you. Here's how you can get them.' This is all tied into consumer goods and marketing.

Ikeda: That is very true. In a speech entitled 'The Role of Religion in a Changing International Society', which you delivered at Soka University in May 1992, you said that all humanity is engulfed in the market economy and you warned that, having become prisoners of the consumer culture and material desires, people face a new crisis of spiritual death.

Cox: The consumer culture trivializes and destroys values such as simplicity and compassion that traditional religions uphold. The market does not reward compassion. It doesn't even know about compassion. Religion can sometimes be lured into marketing itself. But religious institutions should be questioning and restraining the market values without advocating getting rid of the market.

Ikeda: I see. In your speech, you mentioned such contemporary topics as 'insatiable desire' and 'spiritual destruction', and questioned religion's ability to cope with them. I believe that religion today must sincerely deal with these issues and apply the brakes to the culture of greed and spiritual destruction. It must contribute to enabling human beings to live as they should in the modern material civilization.

How can we control the energy of unrestrained greed and channel it towards the creation of good values?

Stimulating False Appetites – The Fantasy of a Market Religion

Cox: Many of modern humanity's desires are not real needs. In their pursuit of profit, market controllers always have to stimulate false appetites.

Ikeda: As you pointed out in your lecture, in sophisticated consumer economics, mass media – such as television – constantly stimulate and expand consumer desires to escalate consumption. Instead of things they really physically need, consumers tend to buy things they *think* they need. Some purchases do have value in enriching and making life more convenient. In many cases, however, they are merely useless objects for which false desires have been artificially stimulated.

Cox: That is true. Such products undercut and trivialize the real values and feelings that make us human. This in turn has a lot to do with the impact of what might be called the commodity culture. A commodity symbolizes happiness or success or love or belonging. But it's a false symbol. It does not impart the things it stands for.

Ikeda: Advertising is awash in commodity-related information, deluding people into thinking that social position and worth as human beings depend on specific objects and brand-name products.

Cox: What I call the 'market religion' is the main rival of the traditional religions of the world. We must question its values and the fictions it is built around. A television commercial is a tiny story. For example, obese people are told that, if they take a certain advertised pill, they will become slender and love will surely come their way at last. People are surrounded by all these false stories.

Ikeda: Because human greed tends towards limitless hyper-trophy, the ability to make wise judgements and the spiritual strength to control desires are absolutely essential.

Buddhist Wisdom as a Way to Revive Spiritual Strength

Ikeda: The German sociologist Ferdinand Tönnies (1855–1936) wrote that vanity needs others as a mirror and that egoism needs others as tools.[1] A fulfilled mind, not the possession of many things, is the primary condition for satisfaction and happiness. The Lotus Sutra teaches us to want little and know satisfaction. If we want little, this controls the hypertrophy of desire that, when it becomes destructive and harmful, is called in Buddhist terms *rāga*, or greed. Controlling desire in such a way as to fulfil one's own life and the lives of others and to become a driving force for happiness is the meaning of the injunction to desire little and know satisfaction.

Cox: The admonition 'Know how much is enough', which I learned in Kyoto, made my whole trip there worthwhile. Like your 'Want little and know satisfaction', it is a vitally important piece of advice for modern humanity.

People who live quite simply are often extraordinarily happy. Of course, I'm not talking about the impoverished. I mean people who are less swayed by the mass-media advertising messages constantly bombarding them. They may not have great wealth, but they are content.

Ikeda: The Buddha's Legacy Teaching Sutra explains that recognizing sufficiency makes life rich, pleasant and tranquil. On the other hand, failing to know satisfaction means that even a life that seems rich is in fact impoverished and dominated by vanity and desires for material things, power and fame. A truly rich person overcomes basic egoism and controls greed, prejudice and antagonism. Such a person works hard to create a spiritual, ethical way of life aiming for the happiness of the self and of others.

Buddhism calls deep-seated, uncontrollable tendencies of life and desires ignorance (*avidyā*). Unless we are courageous enough to reform this state of ignorance, no fundamental solutions to the problems it causes are possible, and we must remain confined in its darkness.

Cox: Escaping from the prison of ignorance requires a revival of spiritual power. Religious values are important to this indispensable undertaking. Because it evokes spontaneous strength from within, Buddhism is going to be absolutely vital to the coming age.

The Buddhist Middle Way of Living

Ikeda: In what is called the Four Departures from the Palace, when he was still the Prince Gautama, Shakyamuni encountered four sights that greatly influenced the course of his life.

Upon leaving by the east gate, he saw an old man. This encounter taught him that whatever lives must grow old. Leaving by the south gate, he came upon a sick man. This meeting convinced him that whatever lives is subject to illness. Upon departing from the west gate, he encountered a corpse.

This showed him that whatever lives must die. Finally, when he left by the north gate, he encountered a monk in training. Observing his tranquillity of form and mind, the prince resolved to abandon secular life to pursue the Way.

Cox: That is a very famous story.

Ikeda: All human beings must age, fall ill and die. No amount of wealth enables us to escape these sufferings. Realizing this convinced the young, affluent and healthy Gautama to don coarse garments and leave the royal palace. He saw that a life of material affluence and freedom from want does not impart real happiness. Indeed, it can be fraught with insecurity, fear, fretfulness and lethargy arising from the fundamental sufferings of birth, ageing, illness and death.

Cox: As I understand it, leaving home in search of enlightenment, Gautama rejected all desire. He entered into a life of harsh asceticism and fasting that, as some sculpture reveals, left him little more than skin and bones. Finding this regimen ineffectual, he sought another kind of training and in doing so discovered the Middle Way.

Some Christian teachings, too, advocate practically perpetual fasting in the hope of eliminating sexual desire. I think this is a mistaken way to try to deal with the situation, although, in the light of the consumer culture's efforts to fan human desire, a certain kind of asceticism makes real sense.

Ikeda: Totally eliminating all desire would be to extinguish mind and body. Buddhist teachings hold that destroying the body extinguishes wisdom (in Japanese the term is *keshin mecchi*). Extreme asceticism is virtually suicide. There was a certain Buddhist school that tried to practise such extreme asceticism. The important thing is the Middle Way that you have mentioned. Veering to neither extreme, the moderation of this Way provides a dynamic way of living that, in accord with the fundamental law of life pervading humanity and the whole cosmos, is radiantly wise and enables us to cope with and overcome the tempests of a constantly changing society. In a dialogue with me, Dr Toynbee said of the Middle Way:

> ... alternatively it can be oriented deliberately to objectives that are right for oneself and are good for one's fellow human beings and for the universe as a whole. I believe that a human being should aim not at the unattainable objective of extinguishing desire but at the attainable and desirable objective of directing desire towards good objectives.[2]

Cox: The way to purify energy and use it to best advantage is to employ it for the good of others.

Ikeda: Exactly. The happiness that we can savour deep inside and that never fades is happiness shared. Nichiren, the founder of Nichiren Buddhism, of which we are devotees, wrote, '"Joy" means that oneself and others experience joy.'[3] Such happiness creates the kinds of joyful bonds that lead to devoted actions for the sake of a friend's smile. Helping each individual to live in this way is the theme that religion must confront today.

Cox: I agree entirely. As the etymology of the word (from Latin *religare*, to retie) indicates, the great role of religion today is to re-form the bonds that connect people. Accomplishing this is one of the areas in which my hopes for SGI are very high.

SGI – Pioneering the Way to a New Religious Reformation

Ikeda: As a well-known specialist in the field, you have published numerous books on religion and secularization, including *The Secular City: Secularization and Urbanization in Theological Perspective* and *Religion in the Secular City: Toward a Postmodern Theology*.

33

Secularization is widely discussed among theologians today, when religion appears to some to be losing its former power in the face of technological and scientific advances, the development of the market economy and urbanization. This loss, however, may really be only an apparent loss. Using your own eyes and ears, you have carried out rigorous surveys focused on diverse religious trends.

Cox: Although these social changes were predicted to marginalize or even cause religion to disappear or lose influence, that did not happen. What happened instead was a revival, a kind of a renaissance, of religion. This was a surprise for many scholars.

Ikeda: Rapid changes in the times and the social environment make people all the more aware of the need for religion. During the latter half of the 1960s, new religious groups attracted by oriental mysticism sprang up on the West Coast of the United States. Latin America witnessed the spread of the popular movement called liberation theology. In 1979, the Iranian Islamic Revolution caught the attention of the world. As is well known, since the collapse of the Soviet Union, the traditional Russian Orthodox Church has revived vigorously.

Cox: The religion revival has taken some good, some bad and some mixed forms. But social change in no way lessens or diminishes the human need for religion.

Ikeda: I agree. My mentor used to say that the more science advances, the more the greatness of Buddhism will be proved. Human existence cannot be explained on the basis of reason alone. While including reason, we must turn our gaze inwards to the inner spirituality – religious nature – that transcends reason. Today the trend is for more and more people to grasp this.

Cox: Religion may take different forms but it persists. The adaptations it makes are one of the most interesting topics of study. I mean by this the ways religions change in the face of challenges and yet retain their core teaching, their dharma, their gospel, or whatever is central to them.

Ikeda: To continue contributing to broader human happiness and social development, a religion must adapt to the changing times. But it must never abandon its essential teachings, its core spirituality. In your understanding of contemporary religions in general, you take a balanced view of these two aspects and have offered SGI much valuable advice in connection with our activities for peace, culture and education.

Cox: SGI has changed a great deal since I first became familiar with it. Though it seemed tragic when it happened, without doubt separation from the sect with which it was formerly associated was the best and most constructive thing that could have happened to SGI. I especially appreciate the work of the Boston Research Center for the 21st Century (BRC), an SGI-affiliated international peace institute, located a few blocks from my home.

Ikeda: Thank you for your comment. When we broke our ties with the sect and initiated new religious reforms, you expressed your hope that SGI would no longer adhere to traditional, ceremonial, closed religious views but, flying the banner of friendship and engaging in exchanges with peoples everywhere, would move in the direction of a future-oriented humanistic religion. Your counsel still encourages us greatly.

We have taken our stand for a religious renaissance with the happiness of the ordinary people as its goal. We strive to determine the nature of religion for a new age that will enable people to live in such a way as to manifest their true humanity.

We also want to discover ways in which religion can contribute to human happiness and social development. I hope that this dialogue will examine these themes from a variety of angles.

35

FOUR

The Age of the Internet: Interplay of Danger and Promise

___

The Role of Religion in the Twenty-First Century

Ikeda: In spite of being closer in material and informational terms, people today exist in a state of spiritual isolation from each other. I consider this a major problem for contemporary society. With their lives devoid of comradeship and intimacy, many people find human relationships savage. Restoring human ties and making local communities, and society more generally, warmly humane are two of religion's most important roles in the twenty-first century.

Cox: I agree. That is why conferences of representatives of the world's religious traditions are so important. Organizations for this are already in place. For instance, in Cambridge, Massachusetts, we have the BRC, with a Buddhist-inspired programme sponsored by SGI. There are Christian groups in Japan and China. Today we need places where we can confer together in non-sectarian terms and will need more of them in the future.

Ikeda: That is very true. Furthermore, I believe that this dialogue with you will have profound significance for the future. As computers improve, the world is rapidly entering an age of sophisticated information technology (IT). Many people consider the Internet an indispensable part of life. Certainly it provides fast access to libraries and museums all over the world: people can display their ideas and artworks worldwide on the Internet and exchange wisdom with strangers in the interest of solving all kinds of problems. Of course, its effects are not always good. In many parts of the globe, the Internet causes incidents and even tragedies.

Cox: Yes, in September 2005, satirical cartoons of the Prophet Muhammad appeared in a small newspaper in Denmark. Related news and images appeared on the Internet, where millions of people all around the world could see them. In horrible reactions, embassies were burned and several people were killed.

Ikeda: It was all very lamentable. Discriminatory remarks made on the Internet cease being expressions of individual opinion and can ignite large-scale antagonism and hatred. Japan has witnessed instances in which complete strangers have come together on the Internet to form suicide pacts.

Cox: Like everything else, the Internet cannot be called a universally beneficent invention. Maybe nothing can.

Ikeda: Today, with unprecedented speed and on an unprecedented scale, people learn of accidents and disasters in remote areas inaccessible to the mass communications media and can extend the hand of assistance. Although it certainly has both positive and negative aspects, undeniably, as a new kind of communication tool, the Internet is seriously changing global informational flow and ideas about the way society ought to be.

Cox: That is very true. In 2002, the late pope, John Paul II, said the Internet has opened up a new world of space for the imagination at the start of the millennium. Like new frontiers in other epochs, cyberspace is accompanied by the sense of adventure but is also full of the interplay of danger and promise.[1]

It opens a space for anybody to display hatred and bigotry – even pornography. Although strangers can meet in cyberspace, I do not think the Internet has necessarily brought people closer together. We must pay attention to both its perilous and its hope-giving elements.

Ikeda: The greater the influence of the Internet becomes, the more energetically the ethics and responsibility of its users come into question. Setting up rules based on reliable ethics and value criteria is indispensable. Another important topic is the way religions can respond and contribute to the Internet society from the ethical and spiritual standpoint.

The Need for Universal Values

Cox: The growth of the Internet makes increasingly clear our need for the universal values that you advocate. Although the Internet draws us all into closer relations, we preserve our different world views, and the perennial problem of how to exchange views through dialogue persists. The Internet has not changed our task or our challenge at all.

Ikeda: I agree. Many religions have striven to transcend personal, class, cultural and ethnic differences in the search for shared universal values. The golden rules of most religions – against taking life, stealing and deceiving – must be the foundation. Buddhism puts special emphasis on compassion. We must reaffirm such universal values as our common heritage and employ them to promote mutual understanding.

Cox: Buddhist compassion is very similar to the central teaching of Christianity, which is love of our neighbour and even of our enemy. For Judaism, on the other hand, the idea of justice is more important than compassion. In the Judaic view, compassion or love without justice becomes mere sentiment.

Ikeda: The Buddhist term *compassion* is defined as relieving suffering and giving joy. This means that being compassionate requires both having a caring heart and struggling against the causes of suffering. In the Nirvana Sutra, thought to have been expounded after the Lotus Sutra by Shakyamuni at the last stage of his life, we find this passage: 'If one befriends another person but lacks the mercy to correct him, one is in fact his enemy. But one who reprimands and corrects an offender is a voice hearer who defends the Buddha's teachings, a true disciple of the Buddha.'[2]

Mere superficial kindness is not the true meaning of either love or compassion. It is the product of indifference. From time to time, we must reprimand and correct people we truly care about. The pure and mighty force of life – the Buddha nature – is inherent in all human beings. People who believe this make clear, firm distinctions between good and bad and consider sincere, honest dealing important. This attitude makes it possible to evoke, cultivate and burnish human dignity. In addition, we must resolutely battle against anything that denigrates or infringes humanity.

Cox: That is a very important point. I think the really central factors are respect and recognition of the image of what Christians call God in all human beings. In different terms, this is human dignity, which must be respected, nurtured, and given an opportunity to grow and flower. Most religious traditions agree on these things. For instance, the Lotus Sutra teaching that the Buddha nature exists in all human beings is one of Buddhism's most important and attractive characteristics.

Ikeda: Religions must reaffirm human dignity, and all humanity must discover and proclaim universal values. The Lotus Sutra teaches that Shakyamuni appeared in this world for the precise purpose of revealing, pointing out and enlightening people to the supreme Buddhist wisdom, which is in all of us. We can safely predict that a major focal point in the new age is going to be devising ways of allowing that wisdom to shine forth and of applying it in real life and society.

Giving Hope to the Unhappy

Ikeda: You have written that, in your late teens, you came to have reservations about any religion that shows no interest in social reform.[3] Certainly the contribution that religion can make to the manifestation of social justice is a matter of extreme importance. Christianity, Islam and Buddhism all believe that such reforms begin with a warm, caring attitude towards people who suffer as a result of social anomalies. My own mentor Josei Toda always said that, if they could be brought together in one room, the founders of the great religions would immediately agree on most things. In other words, they would clarify their goals, do away with useless inter-religious controversy and adopt an elevated position of tolerance.

Cox: I think so, too. St Francis of Assisi (1182?–1276), who lived in the same century as Nichiren, tried to reform society by setting an example of simple living without riches or property and by challenging the Church to curtail its worldly power, influence and wealth.

Whereas St Francis worked by setting an example, other people tried to do it by social reform. In Christian history, the Puritans, fleeing persecution in the search for freedom of religion, came to New England eventually to mandate social reforms. In doing so, however, they made some very serious mistakes.

Ikeda: Holding aloft ideals of religious reform, the Puritans sought religious freedom for themselves but tried to force others to abide by their own doctrines.

Cox: Yes, they did. Once people adopt a mentality of social reform, they become impatient with dissent from their vision of what social reform should be.

Ikeda: This is a trap facing reformers in religious, social, economic and many other fields. Ideals with the noblest goals lose value if imposed forcibly and violently.

Cox: Very true. At the beginning of the twentieth century, Walter Rauschenbusch started his wonderful social gospel movement. A Baptist theologian, he thought social, educational, political and economic institutions should be suffused with what he saw as the Christian view of equality, peace and justice. He was especially concerned about working people. His parish was in a very poor section of New York City called Hell's Kitchen.

Rauschenbusch went from a strictly individual understanding of the meaning of the Christian Gospel to what he called a social gospel that should be applied on all of levels of society.

Ikeda: Religious practice must begin with work among distressed people. In its early formative years, Soka Gakkai was scorned and despised as a group of paupers and sick people because it gave hope and extended the hand of salvation to distressed people in the depths of misery. We are now proud to regard all the criticism and calumny poured down on us then as marks of honour.

Transcending Time and Boundaries – Undercurrents of Conscience

Cox: Rightly so. This is a point I should like to underscore. Even today, when SGI has expanded worldwide, the spirit of its formative days remains vibrantly alive.

But to return to Rauschenbusch: he was very much against war as a way of solving problems and he opposed the First World War throughout its duration. He believed it would create more problems than it solved; he turned out to be right. The way the First World War ended and the subsequent enforced peace did, indeed, create enormous and disruptive problems.

Ikeda: Without a doubt. The tragedies of the First and Second World Wars and the regional conflicts taking place all over the world today make that perfectly clear. Gandhi and Martin Luther King, Jr. both opposed violence because they knew that it spawns a train of endless disaster. Of course, peace cannot be achieved with mere adjustments in systems and mechanisms.

Cox: Rauschenbusch died not long after the end of the First World War. But his important movement has never completely died out. It reappears in different forms now and then, and we may discern some evidence of it in certain Christian movements devoted to environmental concerns and peace. Certainly, as he said himself, Martin Luther King, Jr. was influenced by the social gospel. So was Gandhi.

Ikeda: In his autobiography, Martin Luther King, Jr., who read Rauschenbusch's writings in his youth, wrote this about the role of religion: 'On the one hand I must attempt to change the soul of individuals so that their societies may be changed. On the other I must attempt to change the societies so that the individual soul will have a change. Therefore, I must be concerned about unemployment, slums, and economic insecurity. I am a proud advocate of the social gospel.'[4] As is well known, Gandhi too was deeply concerned about the downtrodden, especially the so-called untouchables of the Indian caste system, whom he called *Harijan*, or God's Children. He renamed *Young India*, a paper he supervised, *Harijan* and organized the *Harijan* Service Committee to work for their liberation and to promote the reconstruction of farming villages.

The most unfortunate people have the greatest right to be happy. People of religion must exert the utmost efforts to help them find happiness. In this spiritual struggle – transcending time and boundaries – the labours of people of religion can create a great undercurrent of conscience, benefiting many people in many places. We should work harder to make this a century free of the tears of grief and sorrow.

The Threat of Apocalyptic Violence

Ikeda: The American psychiatrist Robert Jay Lifton points to the danger of violence resonating with the global chronic anxiety accompanying information acceleration and globalization, especially as centred on the Internet. In modern society, a complicated entwining of various interests and other elements makes problem solving difficult. Some people therefore think it would be simpler to start all over again from scratch. In his analysis of their mental states, Lifton found that Vietnam veterans often felt that local villages were so hopelessly retarded that the only way to save them was to destroy them. He discovered the same kind of attitude in his studies of fanatical terrorists. He calls violence rooted in this mindset apocalyptic and says that, with the help of Internet technology, it has created a global system of apocalyptic violence.

Cox: The world is rife with anomalies and complications that we must persevere to deal with. We cannot hope to attain perfect freedom by eliminating them all at once. As soon as one anomaly

44

is overcome, another pops up to take its place. Confronting and trying to overcome them deepens us spiritually and enables us to contemplate a complex future and move steadily ahead towards solutions, step by step.

Ikeda: Religion's role is to calm impatience and to cultivate a tenacity of will and a reliable, steadfast approach that enables us to stand up against apocalyptic violence.

The Need for Spiritual Organizations that Prize Every Individual

Ikeda: While recognizing the importance of religion, people sometimes need help in persevering in their faith. That is where organizations are useful. In your writings, you have expressed concern at the modern tendency to individualism and have commented on the importance of organizations such as the Buddhist *sangha*, or order.[5]

Cox: One of the basic attractions of religion is bonding with others. One of my teachers once said to me, 'You know, we theologians spend a lot of time studying religions and denominations, but people don't join religions or denominations. They join congregations.'

Ikeda: Educational and intimate exchanges between individuals are a very important element for the practice of faith.

Cox: Yes. People join small groups whose members share their hopes and where they form open, trusting bonds. In my view, although some religions lack it to one extent or another, generally speaking, the congregation is the basic unit of which religions are made up.

Ikeda: In the case of SGI, the central unit is the small discussion group called the *zadankai*. At these meetings, young and old gather to listen to each other's problems, exchange opinions, and offer encouragement. Many people, especially in the United States, are surprised at the successful way *zadankai* form diverse collectives free of concern with ethnicity.

Cox: *Sanghas* of that kind are greatly needed.

Ikeda: Josei Toda considered the Soka Gakkai organization more important than his own life. He always thought of his comrades who, with the courage and dedication of their faith, constantly struggled against the hardships of human existence. People were what made the organization supremely vital to him, and he would gladly have sacrificed his life to make them happy. This passionate determination constantly coursed through his entire being.

The organization is far more than a mere abstraction. It depends on warm-blooded human ties. People who forget individual members' faces are likely to use organizations to their own selfish advantage. If this happens, the evil aspects of organization run wild. A humanistic *sangha* should be constructed to prevent this kind of abuse.

Cox: Absolutely. The individual must always be respected. Perhaps this is the spirit that accounts for the astonishing progress SGI has made.

FIVE

Rapidly Changing Times: Return to the Origins of Religion

Cox: Please allow me to congratulate you on receiving an honorary doctorate from Beijing Normal University on 7 October 2006. I believe this brings to exactly 200 the number of such academic honours that you have received in recognition of your contributions to peace and learning.

Ikeda: Thank you. I regard these honours as indications of praise for the activities and social contributions of SGI members all over the world. They have all been made possible by the education given to me personally by my mentor Josei Toda, who instructed me in many fields of learning for nearly a decade in my youth. Profoundly grateful to him, I am resolved to make further efforts for the sake of peace, culture and education.

Up to this point in our discussions we have examined the ways that established religions are dealing with the challenge of a rapidly changing society, characterized by globalization and information technology. The rise of radical forces in Islam, Christianity and Hinduism is a subject of great concern.

These tendencies are inseparably linked to the phenomenon of returning to the origins – that is to say, the essential doctrines and spirit – of religions. What are your views on such trends?

Cox: Within religions, certain camps always condemn attempts to respond to social change as an abandonment of the essentials of faith. This explains the existence of religious fundamentalism over the past hundred years or so.

Ikeda: Basically, the word 'fundamentalism' originated as an idea associated with specific American Protestant denominations. Though it may be defined in many ways, today it generally refers to people who insist on strict, literal interpretations of religious teachings. Sometimes it is used to refer to exclusivist attitudes that regard certain ideas and propositions as absolute. Usually it conjures up a negative impression of extremism.

Cox: Yes. But, in one form or another, fundamentalist movements exist, not only in Christianity, but also in all the traditional religions of the world. A course I taught at Wellesley showed that, though very different in many other ways, the fundamentalists of all religions have some things in common. The most radical Islamist groups are more opposed to moderate, liberal Muslims than to the West. They struggle against the West only secondarily. They see the United States as supporting people who are not true 'Muslims'.

Ikeda: In other words, their attacks are essentially directed inside and not outside their religious tradition.

Cox: Yes. Some forms of fundamentalism are dangerous since they can become narrow and very exclusivist. On the other hand, fundamentalism is not entirely useless because it reminds us that, in making adaptations, we must keep the core of a traditional continuity in mind. In this sense, the *traditionalist* makes a more positive contribution than the *fundamentalist*.

48

In all religions, traditionalists serve a genuine purpose in the overall picture.

Fundamentalism as a Modern Phenomenon

Ikeda: I see. A basic Buddhist doctrine – called *zuiho-bini* in Japanese – is to abide by local contemporary customs as long as essential Buddhist teachings are observed. To forget them or to deviate from those fundamentals, however, is seen as putting the cart before the horse.

Therefore, in responding to the changing times, we of Soka Gakkai strive to preserve the continuity of our core faith while taking local traditions into consideration. As you know, in 1992, in an unprecedented act of religious mayhem, the clergy excommunicated Soka Gakkai, at one stroke abandoning ten million believers. By flaunting their sense of superiority over lay believers, the clergy simultaneously exposed their own bigotry and essential lack of conscience. As you once pointed out, breaking with them was the best thing that could have happened to SGI. For one thing, it proved that Soka Gakkai represents legitimate Nichiren Buddhism, which teaches the equality and dignity of all human beings.

The incident also provided a chance for Soka Gakkai to grow and develop into a group more open to society and the world. The number of countries and regions in which we are active has consequently grown from 115 at that time to 192 today.

But to return to the mainstream of our discussion, how do fundamentalists and traditionalists differ?

Cox: Traditionalism is a movement – sometimes a large one – promoted by members of a religious community who are attached to customary ways of prayer, liturgies, festivals, holidays and food regulations inherited from ancestors. Fundamentalists, on the other hand, are people who go back to a particular period or scripture and very selectively retrieve certain parts for revival in contemporary battles. We often forget that fundamentalism is a relatively modern phenomenon. It differs from traditionalism. Indeed many traditionalists are horrified by what fundamentalists are doing.

Ikeda: As has been pointed out by others, in narrow, simplistic forms, such ideas are likely to nurture violence.

Cox: We have witnessed the emergence in virtually every religious tradition of something like a fundamentalist wing that sometimes includes a violent sub-sector. A few Christian fundamentalists tend to believe that violence against abortion clinics is permissible. They have even bombed them and shot and killed doctors and staff members; they try to justify such actions as saving the lives of unborn children. Elements among fundamentalist conservative Jews are perfectly willing to use violence not only against their Arab neighbours, but also against their own people. Indeed, one ultra-conservative fundamentalist Jew assassinated the prime minister of Israel. And, of course, a segment of the conservative wing of Islam employs violence against fellow Muslims.

Religious violence is alarming. But in my opinion, it is not going to increase or do enormous harm.

The Error of Applying the Same Standards to All Cultures

Ikeda: In a sense, after the collapse of the Soviet Union, Islamic fundamentalism became the West's new problem. Samuel P. Huntington's 1993 proclamation of clashes of civilizations is surely not unrelated to this way of thinking about the times.

Cox: When coupled with political movements or motivations or enlisted in political causes, fundamentalism becomes very dangerous indeed.

Ikeda: Yes, it does. But many people attribute solely to religious teaching the causes of violence and conflict that actually have a complex background of politico-social conditions. It is a reckless attitude, because these unstable conditions are partly caused by those who simple-mindedly insist on the danger of religion.

Cox: Yes. Although I disagree with the 'clash of civilizations' idea, Huntington makes at least one convincing point when he writes that different civilizations have different profiles and that we must not try to homogenize them. Instead of imposing Western views on them, we should encourage different cultures to develop within their own dynamic, drawing on their own resources and religion or religions. Although the part of his book expressing these ideas has not been widely read or appreciated, it makes the good point that we should listen, appreciate differences and look for more than similarities and commonalities.

Ikeda: Today the need to listen to each other, recognize our differences and prize diversity is greater than it has ever been. In the moving terms used by Nigerian Nobel literature laureate Wole Soyinka when we met and engaged in conversation, the simplest justice is not to do to others things you would not like done to you. He went on to say that the basis of all justice is the ability to imagine oneself in the other party's position. Without empathy and compassion, there can be no true justice.

In his explanation of the concept of *ren*, or humaneness, in the dialogue he and I conducted, Tu Weiming of Harvard, a foremost expert on Chinese philosophy, stated the same idea in the Confucian formulation: 'Do not do unto others what you would not want others to do unto you.' He also quoted from the Analects: 'In order to establish ourselves, we help others to establish themselves; in order to expand ourselves, we help others expand themselves.'

This brings to mind the Buddhist concept of compassion expressed in the dictum that life is dear to all living creatures and that, by comparing them to ourselves, we must neither kill nor cause others to kill. This instructs us in the importance of empathy-inspired caring and respect for others. The role of religion is to train the imaginative faculty to acknowledge and empathize with the sufferings of others.

Cox: Yes – the imagination and the desire to go on asking questions. I remember seeing bumper stickers on the cars of, presumably, fundamentalist Christians that proclaimed, 'I have found the answer!' For me, a better bumper sticker would say, 'I'm still asking the question.' And as long as I am asking the question, I remain fully human.

Start Listening Now

Ikeda: That is true. The humility to go on asking the question is the starting point for dialogues connecting different cultures and civilizations.

Absolutely nothing can justify shocking acts of terror such as the attacks on the United States on 11 September 2001. But we must go on asking the questions and trying to discover why such tragedies occur and what inflames people with so much hatred that they are willing to give their own lives in acts of terrorism.

Cox: The events of 9/11 shattered the dangerous myth of American invincibility. Separated from the rest of the world by two oceans, we were militarily and economically powerful. Then suddenly in one day the World Trade Center in New York, the great icon of our economic power, and the Pentagon in

Washington, the symbol of our military power, were struck by a force previously unknown to most Americans.

Ikeda: I sympathize with the profound grief and rage aroused in the minds of many by the 9/11 attacks. One of the most promising graduates of our own Soka University was among the approximately 3,000 people who died that day. At the same time, however, I am deeply pained at the large numbers of innocent lives lost in Afghanistan in events after the attacks. Revenge for violent terrorism sets up an endless chain of violence. For the sake of the peaceful world we all want, we must investigate and eradicate the social factors that give rise to terrorism.

Cox: Terrorism is generally the weapon of the weak. It is used by people who feel they have no other way of asserting their rights or escaping from oppression. It is not big countries with big armies but smaller minority groups lacking substantial armaments that resort to terrorism, which can be said to be societally induced. Its underlying causes are not just poverty, hunger and unemployment, but to a very large extent, the sense that individuals, their country and its culture are not being afforded the dignity and recognition they deserve.

Ikeda: The chain of violence did not suddenly emerge on 11 September. It relates to both past and future. The causal factors behind modern terrorism have been evolving over a long period of history and involve a tangle of world political, economic and religious conditions. Consequently, although it may seem a long-winded method, the only way to solve the problem is through steady perseverance. Of one thing I am absolutely certain: choosing violence as a way of dealing with terrorism will spell disaster for future generations.

Cox: I think 9/11 is a very good example of a terrorist attack by people lacking weaponry: they did not even have their own airplanes but had to hijack some. It was an attack on the United

States not as the principal enemy, but as the ally of the Muslim powers they were opposing. Of course, the terrorists resented the presence of American troops in Saudi Arabia near the holy shrines at Mecca and Medina. Nonetheless, it was not a conflict of civilizations.

Though the major tension today is often among its various expressions, we must appreciate the internal dynamic within Islam and its different parties, schools of thought and tendencies. We must not see it as one single, ominous picture.

Ikeda: In a dialogue we conducted, the Iranian Professor Majid Tehranian and I discussed Islamic traditional culture and religion. From our talks, I came to see the need to devote more effort to knowing and understanding the diversity and appeal of the Islamic world.

You once told me you hoped that Buddhism could bridge the gap between Christianity and Islam. In your essay published in *Religion, the Missing Dimension of Statecraft*, you wrote, 'One of the most intriguing features of Buddhism for anyone interested in religious sources for conflict resolution is that it arose precisely as a method for coping with just such dilemmas.'[1]

In my own way, I hope to satisfy your expectation. Easing global tensions is the way to deal with the causes of terrorism. It cannot be done overnight. But we can begin at once engaging in dialogue and listening to each other.

Cox: Indeed we can. Sincere exchanges of opinion at a conference by representatives of three of the major religions – Christianity, Buddhism and Islam – would produce interesting results. All three would be enriched by the experience of learning from each other.

SIX

Courageous Heroes of Non-Violence

<hr />

Ikeda: Several events made 2007 an important pivotal time in the drive forwards for peace. The Pugwash Conferences, where world scientists gathered together to work for the abolition of nuclear weapons, and to which the late Dr Joseph Rotblat devoted his life, marked the fiftieth anniversary of their inception, as did the International Atomic Energy Agency (IAEA), which promotes the peaceful use of atomic energy and strives to prohibit its conversion to military purposes. In November 2006, Mohamed ElBaradei, the second director general of the organization, discussed its future outlook with me.

The year 2007 also had special significance for SGI as the fiftieth anniversary of Josei Toda's Declaration for the Abolition of Nuclear Weapons, the source of our pacifist movement. We determined to make this anniversary a fresh starting point for still greater solidarity among the ordinary peoples of the world.

Cox: I sincerely hope that the SGI peace movement will continue to develop. The issue of nuclear weapons is of enormous concern to me and should be so to everyone. The non-proliferation treaty we now have was signed by both nuclear and non-nuclear nations. This is rarely mentioned. Non-nuclear nations have agreed not to develop nuclear arms, and nuclear states have agreed to dismantle their nuclear arsenals. But the nuclear states have not even started dismantling. At a meeting in New York in the spring of 2005, nuclear and non-nuclear participants came to the conclusion that they could do nothing and went home. That fiasco of a conference accomplished nothing at all.

In 2005, in the hope that, working together, religious communities might be able to accomplish something, we organized an interfaith alliance to prevent nuclear war. Surveys have shown that most of the people of the United States support nuclear disarmament.

Ikeda: On the basis of a shared advocacy of respect for life, all religions – Buddhism, Christianity and Islam alike – should cooperate and engage in dialogues on nuclear weapons. As the only nation in the world ever to have suffered a nuclear attack, Japan has an especially grave mission and great responsibility in this respect.

Convinced that this is true, we of SGI have undertaken various anti-nuclear projects. For example, we have held an exhibition entitled 'Nuclear Arms: Threat to Our World' in many parts of the globe. In 1998, SGI Youth Division members presented a petition to the United Nations for the elimination of nuclear weapons signed by thirteen million people. In September 2006, in the light of increasing nuclear-related tensions, I proposed the establishment of a UN decade of nuclear abolition action by the world's peoples. Fear of nuclear arms has a tighter grip on the world today than ever before. That is why we must act now.

Cox: Yes, but the problem is that, surrounded by other crises, people sometimes forget how utterly central the challenge of nuclear weapons is.

Ikeda: Or if aware of the problem, they fail to act.

Counter to expectations, confusion in the post-Cold War world has only worsened. Analyses have been made of causes for this, such as changes in the world order, the economics of warfare and injustice and poverty caused by globalization. While taking these analyses into consideration, however, we should once again also focus on inner issues related to the human spirit and human thought because it is in human life and the human mind that we can find the ultimate cause of and solution to the problem of indifference to the sufferings of others as well as physical violence and such structural violence as poverty.

Cox: In this connection, I am reminded of what Pope John Paul II said in his New Year message for 2002: 'No peace without justice.' I am in total agreement with the idea that we must pursue justice if we want peace. Pacifist movements and peace organizations are often so focused on actual instances of violence and belligerence that they lose sight of the various forms of injustice that are almost always the underlying causes.

Ikeda: That is true. In his declaration against nuclear weapons, Josei Toda argued that all people have the right to live and that anyone or anything that would deprive them of that right is evil and satanic. Nothing could justify a repetition of the tragedies of Hiroshima and Nagasaki in which hundreds of thousands of precious lives were lost. In *The Republic*, Plato said that throughout human history the strong and victorious have monopolized justice. In fact, however, winners have not always had justice on their sides. True justice must accommodate the peace and happiness of the common people. Making them unhappy, even in the name of ostensibly the most noble causes, is unjust.

Nuclear Arms – Symbols of Escalating Violence

Cox: At the end of the Second World War, in the name of justice, Allied forces conducted horrendous, inexcusable forms of aerial warfare at Dresden and Hamburg, almost entirely against civilians. When people look back now, they wonder how we could have done it. I was only a boy at the time, but I remember hearing of thousand-sortie raids destroying German cities just as the war was ending. Many people speculate that the real aim was not so much a blow against Germany as a desire to demonstrate American air power to the Soviets. I suspect that the bombing of Nagasaki and Hiroshima had a similar motivation. It is also possible that the Americans wanted to end the war as quickly as possible before the Russians could enter northern Japan. Hard facts show that atrocities escalate as war progresses. In general, violence that is comparatively restrained at the outset of hostilities intensifies with time.

Ikeda: Owing to the fearsome nature of war and something equally frightening in human nature, repeated instances of small-scale violence numb people to greater violence.

Cox: Events at the small village of Guernica in the Spanish Civil War provide a classic example. The air raid on Guernica took only about sixty lives – a small number compared to other greater atrocities. Nonetheless, the fact that the victims were mostly civilians sparked a huge worldwide outcry and a classic painting by Picasso. At Hiroshima from 60,000 to 80,000 people died in a moment. Perhaps more than 100,000 died at Dresden. But in these later cases, the outcry was more subdued. So, as violence constantly gains momentum, we lose our capacity for understanding the nature of its evil.

Ikeda: As is related in the 2003 film *The Fog of War: Eleven Lessons from the Life of Robert S. McNamara*, once war has started, the process whereby ends are thought to justify means gets out of hand. Reason is of no assistance; humans do evil with the intention of doing good. These are two of the conclusions that McNamara, secretary of defence during one phase of the Vietnam War, drew from his experiences in conflicts with Japan, Vietnam and the Soviet Union.

Progress in the production of armament plays the role of catalyst in the limitless advance of violence. Such progress has now made it possible to press a button and wreak havoc on some place far, far away. Technological advances have not only spawned power to cause great indiscriminate bloodshed, but have also created an immense physical and psychological gap between the harmer and the harmed, thus dulling the distress inherent in the act of killing. Nuclear weapons symbolize this evolution.

The Manhattan Project's Lesson for the Present

Cox: At Los Alamos, when the American atomic bomb was being developed, J. Robert Oppenheimer and his colleagues believed the Nazis were already producing a similar bomb. The American team was eager to perfect their device before the Germans. They worked very hard on the Manhattan Project, the biggest organized scientific enterprise in history. The whole team was enormously excited to be on this scientific cutting edge and working for the good cause of getting the jump on the Nazis. Later, however, when it became clear – at least to some of them – that the Nazis were nowhere near producing an atomic bomb, they started wondering about the advisability of pursuing the project further. But only one scientist actually left Los Alamos.

Ikeda: Three attitudes are said to have prevailed among the scientists working on the Manhattan Project:

1   Complete indifference to the political uses to which the results of their research would be put.

59

2 Rationalization of the project for various reasons in spite of doubts about its goals.
3 Conscientious disinclination to continue the work once its true goals were discovered.

Joseph Rotblat, secretary-general and president of the Pugwash Conferences, adopted the third position. In a dialogue he and I shared, Professor Rotblat explained in detail the troubles he encountered because of his stance. At one point he was actually suspected of spying.

Cox: Yes, I have heard of the incident. Professor Rotblat explained his reasons in a very moving article in the *Bulletin of the Atomic Scientists* called 'Leaving the Bomb Project'.

Ikeda: Professor Rotblat discussed with me why many scientists remained at Los Alamos:

> The justification offered most often was that they pursued their research for the sake of inquiry into pure basic science. In other words, they were intensely eager to actually prove the theoretical calculations and predictions they had made. It was the feeling of these scientists that society should enter into a discussion about the use of nuclear bombs only after the nuclear experiments.[1]

Cox: When the Los Alamos scientists tested the bomb in the desert at Alamogordo, New Mexico, and saw how powerful it was, some of them began to have real doubts. They advised against dropping it on a city. To demonstrate possession of this fearsome weapon, they proposed dropping it on something else, such as an uninhabited island. But the decision was made to drop it on Hiroshima and even to drop a second bomb, in clear illustration of how violence gains momentum.

Ikeda: Witnessing the tests that demonstrated the bomb's horrendous destructive power, Oppenheimer is said to have been reminded of a passage from the Hindu epic *Bhagavad Gita*: 'I am become death, destroyer of worlds . . .'

Cox: The biography of Oppenheimer, *American Prometheus: The Triumph and Tragedy of J. Robert Oppenheimer* by Kai Bird and Martin J. Sherwin, describes his farewell to Los Alamos. In very significant terms, addressing a huge gathering that had assembled to say goodbye to him, he said that he and his associates had a right to be proud of their work, but that, if atomic bombs were to become part of the arsenals of nations to use in war or to threaten war, the day would come when men would curse the name of Los Alamos.

The people in charge tried to get him to work on America's hydrogen bomb, but he refused. And that was why the military and the politicians ruined his career. Oppenheimer never recovered from the great inner agony that his struggle with his conscience caused him.

Ikeda: He must have felt a tremendous responsibility for the bombings of Hiroshima and Nagasaki. Indeed, though caught between politics and science, he devised practical measures to prevent nuclear expansion from driving humanity to extinction. After the Second World War, he proposed international supervision of nuclear weapons and opposed the development of the hydrogen bomb. Ultimately, swept up in the seas of politics, he lost his public position and suffered terribly. The course of his later life is highly instructive not just for scientists, but for all of us.

Cox: I agree. Once when using *American Prometheus* as a class text, I asked my students to imagine themselves as young, fresh PhD physicists in 1943. What would they have done if Robert Oppenheimer, a leader in their field, had asked them to come to Los Alamos and join the greatest, most exciting enterprise in the history of science, one that would both serve national interests and possibly make future war impossible? Most of my students said they would have gone with him.

Three Great Human Rights Champions Who Reformed the World

Ikeda: The hypothetical situation you presented to your students is very significant. For scientists, as for everyone else, ambitious or not, difficult problems arise when human ethics come into conflict with professional duty and responsibility. In his *Politics as a Vocation*, Max Weber argues that a true politician neither clings to his own beliefs and ideals, refusing all responsibility for results in the actual world, nor claims that beliefs and ideals are unnecessary so long as results are good. A true politician challenges reality tenaciously with a firm and noble belief that enables him to persist and say, 'but still', no matter how difficult the situation or adverse the conditions. I think that people like Mahatma Gandhi, Martin Luther King, Jr. and Nelson Mandela, who reformed the world without abandoning their ideals, are outstanding representatives of the best of humanity.

Cox: Gandhi, King and Mandela drew on different religious resources; but their underlying ideas were very similar and resemble what Quakers call the 'voice of God'. This widely recognized concept was the basis of all their great achievements.

Ikeda: The faith that enabled them to say 'but still' under the most trying circumstances was profoundly religious.

Cox: Because of an indwelling spirit – the inner Buddha or the image of God – in all of us, our humanity must never be violated. Even more important, we must actively promote peace, reciprocity and mutual understanding to prevent hatred and aggression.

Ikeda: The Lotus Sutra – the quintessential Buddhist teaching – identifies all life with the Buddha itself and holds up as an example for religious discipline a bodhisattva named Never Disparaging. He tells everyone, 'I have profound reverence for you. I would never dare treat you with disparagement or arrogance. Why? Because you are all practising the bodhisattva way and are certain to attain Buddhahood.'[2] Although people ridiculed him and attacked him with sticks and stones, he simply went about bowing to them and continued his non-violent practice. Buddhists identify the struggles of Gandhi, King and Mandela with the attitude of this bodhisattva. I have had the honour of meeting Mandela on two occasions. Although I never met either Gandhi or King personally, I have met some of their friends and disciples, including, of course, you.

Cox: I knew only King personally but I am an admirer of all three. I am continually astonished at what Nelson Mandela was able to achieve. Throughout all those years in prison, he avoided bitterness. Though deprived of his leadership status, when he came out of prison, instead of being resentful or vengeful, he was phenomenally magnanimous and generous. He wanted to include the white minority within the new South Africa and managed to make the transition from an apartheid society to a racially inclusive society with amazingly little violence and bloodshed. How South Africa went from what it was to what it is now provides one of the most inspiring and amazing stories of our time.

Ikeda: Mandela was aiming for a rainbow country with equality for all races. Instead of taking revenge on white people, he set up the Truth and Reconciliation Commission to console the victims by laying bare the truth about past instances of violence without pursuing the guilt of the perpetrators. This was his method of attaining reconciliation. Not everyone was satisfied. Some black people were displeased; some white people strenuously opposed digging up the past. But President Mandela, a man of iron will, knew that even after injustice had been exposed and cast out, restoring stability and justice would be a task more difficult than fighting against injustice. A man of courage in the truest sense of the word, Mandela was a rare combination of the ability to pull down an old system and build a new society.

Cox: Yes, Gandhi, King and Mandela were all very courageous. The courage I observed in Martin Luther King, Jr. never flinched even in the face of angry attacks. His was not the bravery of the warrior who kills enemies in battle. He knew how to solve difficult situations non-violently. This takes far more courage.

Ikeda: Gandhi and King were living refutations of the mistaken notion that non-violence is cowardly non-resistance. For them, non-violence meant direct action pointing out injustice to societies that preferred to ignore it and to fall back on false stability. Inevitably, such courageous action evokes antipathy and oppression from ruling powers. This is why non-violence takes courage. As many psychologists indicate, violence is often actually a manifestation of cowardice. King perceived the connection between fear and violence and urged us to overcome the sickness of timorousness. Gandhi, too, insisted that cowards lack a sense of justice.

Cox: Curing cowardice involves a firm belief in the possibility that people and their attitudes can change. This belief is behind the Christian teaching of rebirth; that is, adopting a really fresh, new outlook. Radical change in people is possible; we are not fated to remain as we are.

Ikeda: The theme of my novel *The Human Revolution* is that a great revolution on the part of the individual can change the fate of a nation and of all humanity. This idea derives from the philosophy and spirit of the Lotus Sutra to the effect that limitless possibilities are inherent in the life of each individual. The Lotus Sutra further teaches that changes in a single life can reform the whole environment.

In the ways in which they lived, Gandhi, King and Mandela showed that, far from being petty creatures, human beings have the power to change the world.

Cultivating True Tolerance and Faith as a Spiritual Foundation

Cox: The essential element in the creation of a peaceful world will take us beyond tolerance. Many people misinterpret tolerance as permissiveness: allowing others to do as they like without interference but not necessarily appreciating their actions. Actually, however, we must go further than this. Tolerance is better than intolerance, but it is not nearly enough. To create a truly peaceful world, we must actively appreciate others, welcome them and affirm their status as persons.

Ikeda: I agree completely. Going beyond non-interference and actively appreciating others are of the greatest importance. We must work together actively to generate the kind of tolerance that, going a step further, welcomes diversity and general development by mutually learning from differences.

The SGI charter stresses the importance of tolerance coupled with recognition and appreciation of diversity. True tolerance is the spiritual foundation on which to build and develop mutual understanding and friendship through mind-to-mind exchanges and stronger bonds of sympathy that transcend different value criteria and social backgrounds. In my view, religion in this century should provide the sources of spiritual strength that make this possible.

SEVEN

The Future of China and India: Great Spiritual Heritages

Cox: I am especially interested in the future of China and India. Their relationship to what we loosely call the West is going to be one of the most central issues in forming the future of the world over the next twenty or thirty years. You started to have amicable relationships with them at an early period.

Ikeda: The proud, venerable, spiritual and cultural traditions of both have had a great impact on humanity. Today, their astonishing economic development has come into the spotlight and is strongly affecting the world. With their vast populations – 1.3 billion for China and 1.1 billion for India – their global presence is certain to become increasingly important.

Cox: The ancient and abundant Chinese and Indian cultural heritages interest me more than their power to influence. It would be a terrible loss to all human civilization if these two countries simply followed Western models of modernization and techno-centrism and as a result lost their ancient spiritual heritages for good.

Ikeda: I agree. Exclusive pursuit of technical and scientific development and economic and material prosperity must inevitably lead to an impasse. For the sake of peaceful symbiosis, humanity needs to devise values that engender deeper harmony and solidarity. In our dialogue mentioned earlier, Professor Tu Weiming spoke of a Confucian renaissance as part of a programme to re-evaluate traditional Chinese philosophy.

While mainly urban China undergoes rapid, dramatic changes in economic and social environments, there is a strong tendency among the people to seek traditional spirituality. A new development in this connection is the Chinese government's project to establish Confucius institutes in many parts of the world.

Cox: China is one of the many nations troubled by internal conflict and antagonism. Vast differences separate elites, who are able to profit from recent development, and the multitudinous, poor, working people. Real struggles and class clashes are happening there.

Ikeda: Undeniably, in any country sudden social change generates economic discrepancies and social instability. Furthermore, economic development is accompanied by problems connected with things such as energy consumption, food and environmental concerns. This occurs in Japan as well.

Cox: True. At some point, and I think quite soon, China must work on internal justice issues. Unfortunately, the current leadership has ignored the Chinese cultural and religious heritage. Nonetheless, as a result of recent relaxation of cultural strictures, religious movements and the practice of traditional faiths are emerging. Christianity, too, is growing very rapidly, albeit in an intensely Chinese form that in no way replicates Western expressions and models. Although the biggest movement is one called the Jesus Family, there are many others as well. All are different, and none has any desire to just be an extension of Western Christian thought or institutional structure.

Ikeda: In many areas, the Chinese people are re-examining and reviving their traditions. One current of this revival involves the idea of the unity of heaven and humanity, which Professor Tu and I discussed in connection with the Confucian renaissance. Some time ago, in a dialogue I shared with him, the noted Chinese scholar Ji Xianlin said of this concept, 'I contend that heaven and humankind are one . . . "Heaven" refers to nature, and for humankind to be "one" with nature means that people must seek to understand, live in harmony with, and cease to oppose or fight against the natural world.'

Cox: The concept of the unity of heaven and humanity points to a way to make us more humane. Born weak creatures, we are socialized into human beings. The power generated in the socialization process can be used destructively or in forms emphasizing caring and compassion. One of the most profoundly interesting and valuable teachings of Buddhism, the quintessence of oriental wisdom, widens the family of life by emphasizing caring not just for human beings, but for all life forms. Christianity places less emphasis on this attitude, the importance of which is certain to increase in the years to come.

Ikeda: I think so, too. This is one of the reasons why many intellectuals and scientists are now turning their attention towards oriental – including Buddhist – views of nature and the cosmos.

Cox: The information revolution has come to India – the birthplace of Buddhism – in a very big way, as people are drawn into the computer and outsourcing industry. In terms of religion, India has always been a heterogeneous mixture of a hundred kinds of Hindus plus Muslims, Christians, Sikhs and a small number of Buddhists. All of these religions interact with each other. In some ways, India provides an example of a successful, religiously pluralistic society. In spite of frequent bloody clashes, in general Indians of different religious traditions live side by side harmoniously.

69

Ikeda: Yes, humanity has much to learn from the wisdom of harmony and symbiosis evolved by India's tradition of religious diversity. Oriental philosophy, including the Chinese concept of the harmony of heaven and humanity, can contribute to the creation of new global ethics to serve as a model of symbiosis among individuals, between humanity and nature, and among nations. In political and economic terms, China and India, together with the United States, will be the main participants in a new world order.

In October 1997, I delivered a speech at the Rajiv Gandhi Institute for Contemporary Studies entitled 'A New Humanism for the Coming Century'. In it, I discussed the importance of those three nations as a kind of global triad. Today, cooperation among the three nations is even more vital to a stable global order.

Sino-American Relations and the Importance of Dialogue for Peace

Cox: The future of Sino-American relations is an open question. Some people in America view China as potentially their biggest economic, political – and perhaps even military – rival.

It is inevitable that, given the economic power of the United States and of China, there will be intense rivalry at the economic level. No doubt about it. I hope there will be no military rivalry. I believe that, at this point, the Chinese leadership and the American leadership are wise enough to know how to avoid it.

Ikeda: Yes, I believe so, too. The existence of rivalry explains the great need for dialogue, especially among top leaders. In finding solutions to the problems, leaders of the world must resolutely and indomitably reject hard power in favour of soft power only. If they adopt such an approach as their starting premise, engage their best intelligence and explore all options, they cannot fail to find a way.

Thinking of Sino-American relations recalls how, in July 1971, former US Secretary of State Henry Kissinger astonished the world by crossing the Himalayas to make a lightning-quick, top-secret visit to Beijing. His meetings with Premier Zhou Enlai on that occasion caused a major turnaround in relations between China and the United States. When I met Dr Kissinger in Washington, DC, in January 1975, I proposed the following three basic points for building international cooperation.

1 Give precedence to the opinions of the people of weak countries over the advantages of strong nations.
2 Avoid using military force to solve problems and rely on negotiations instead.
3 Always base specific negotiations for peaceful solutions on discussions between the involved parties.

He entirely agreed with my proposals.

In September 1974, at a time when relations between China and the Soviet Union were becoming strained, as a private citizen, I discussed the importance of peace with Alexei N. Kosygin, then Soviet premier. In December of the same year, I held similar discussions with Premier Zhou Enlai. On these visits to the Soviet Union and China, I was made painfully aware that the world situation obscured the clear, universal desire for peace.

Cox: For the sake of peace in the future, I favour maximum intellectual exchange among university students and faculties and among religious leaders. A great deal of this is going on now, and I hope we continue to build on and amplify it.

Personal Diplomacy for Sino-Japanese Reconciliation

Ikeda: I agree. Convinced that exchanges at the educational level create a reliable foundation for peace and amity, I visited

71

Beijing University on my first visit to China in 1974. Since then, on my ten trips to China, I have made a determined effort to visit universities at every opportunity to deepen exchanges. Soka University was the first Japanese educational institution officially to welcome exchange students from the new China. I am delighted to say that now, for the good of the whole world, large numbers of students from both sides are enthusiastically building bridges between our two countries. One of our first Chinese exchange students, in the role of secretary of the organization, attended a recent meeting of the China–Japan Friendship Association at which association president Song Jian and I discussed the future of Sino-Japanese amicable cooperation.

Cox: That is a good illustration of how educational exchanges bear fruit. To my delight, in the spring of 2006, Soka University joined Harvard and Tokyo University in opening offices in Beijing.

You have always been very interested in China and were visiting and preparing the way for a reconciliation long before anybody else. In fact, your efforts in this direction caused you considerable trouble, I believe.

Ikeda: In 1968, before an audience of about 20,000 students I proposed the normalization of Sino-Japanese relations. In those days, the domestic mood in Japan was such that any politician advocating friendly relations with China put his life in danger. Later, as a man of religion, I was criticized for visiting a country that rejected religion. Nonetheless, I was convinced that friendly relations with China were indispensable to the stability of Japan and all Asia. As I learned from staff members years later, at the time, Zhou Enlai was interested in and deeply sympathetic with the Soka Gakkai movement. The existence of a great leader such as him was very fortunate for us. Integrity, not scheming, is the most important part of diplomacy.

Cox: I respect and rejoice in the work you did. It seems to have borne important results. I am glad you acted on your convictions, even when it meant going against the current.

Ikeda: Thank you for saying so. But, my own contributions aside, Sino-Japanese relations are certainly very important. To win the trust of Asian nations and to contribute to world peace on the basis of dialogue diplomacy while taking advantage of its traditional culture and techno-scientific abilities, Japan must develop into a cultural and environmental nation.

Cox: As far as relations with the United States are concerned, Japan has been more than cooperative and cautious. In a way, the time has come for Japan, without belligerence and excessive self-assertion, to evolve its own way, drawing on important cultural traditions developed over millennia.

Open Discourse Between Wise People

Ikeda: I agree. Until now, the Japanese have subordinated their deepest beliefs to the reckless pursuit of economic growth. They must now begin pursuing spiritual satisfaction.

Cox: Jesus said that man does not live by bread alone. In other words, spiritual enrichment is indispensable to happiness. When I was a child, my mother told me that, if I had two pennies, I should spend one on bread and one on a flower – perhaps a chrysanthemum. The two are equally important: bread to nourish the body and beauty in the form of flowers to nourish the soul.

Ikeda: This charming and philosophical piece of advice vividly reflects your mother's poetic mind and wisdom. I feel that our own dialogue is both open and rewardingly poetic. So, too, was

73

the discussion of Eastern and Western intellect that, transcending differences of rank, took place more than 2,000 years ago between the Greek king Milinda and the Indian sage Nāgasena.

From the very beginning, Nāgasena insisted that their discussion be conducted as between equal sages instead of in the framework of royal authoritarianism. He went on to describe the modesty and open nature of discourse between wise people: 'Your majesty, when the wise converse, whether they become entangled by their opponents' arguments or extricate themselves, whether they or their opponents are convicted of error, whether their own superiority or that of their opponents is established, nothing in all this can make them angry. Thus, your majesty, do the wise converse.'[1] In other words, the dialogue of the wise is honest and sincere and is conducted in an open spirit.

Cox: We can overcome barriers of nation, ethnic group, culture and religion and bring the whole world together only on the basis of this kind of openness.

Ikeda: It is our task to devise ways of going beyond mere exchanges of words and to realize a true dialogue that creates pacifist values. In religious as in other discussions, those seated around the table often find that disagreements prevent their coming together. This is why, to be fruitful, dialogue demands both wisdom and patience.

Cox: It is a very important point. The Harvard Center for the Study of World Religions – where I serve on the advisory board – is preparing to initiate a new programme to invite people to participate in more candid dialogues. Instead of just emphasizing the things that we have in common, we want to be free to speak about the elements that we disagree on, but in an atmosphere of acceptance and listening. One person would have to formulate his or her viewpoint in a way that others, while still disagreeing, would find convincing. This approach would result in very interesting discussions.

Sometimes dialogue evades difficult basic issues that must be faced. This is why we must move into a new stage of dialogue where we respect, seek and nurture common beliefs and practices but also speak candidly to each other about our differences. In the long run, if we learn how to do this in the right way, it will strengthen, not weaken, cooperation.

Ikeda: As you say, after agreement on shared elements, we must move on to recognize and evaluate our differences. Listening carefully to others has several salutary effects. First, it enables us to discover deeper levels in the people we listen to. Second, it leads to self-discovery and the deepening and broadening of our own thought and philosophical bases. In dialogues conducted in this way, both parties discover new horizons of cooperation. Because it opens new paths for dialogue, I value the work being done by the Harvard Center for the Study of World Religions. By moving onto this new stage, in an atmosphere of mutual respect and enlightenment, diverse religions such as monotheistic Christianity and Islam on one hand, and Buddhism, Hinduism, Taoism, and Confucianism with their Indian and Chinese roots on the other, can be expected to reinforce the spirit of cooperation. Dialogue must be the royal road to mutual understanding and trust.

Cox: One of my favourite thinkers, the Jewish philosopher Martin Buber, once said, 'Life itself is dialogue.' In dialogue we not only encounter 'the other', we also encounter ourselves. You could even say – and I certainly would – that we *become human* in dialogue. My principal exemplar, Martin Luther King, Jr., might have said that in a world of nuclear weapons, the only choice is dialogue or extinction. Let us choose dialogue and life.

EIGHT

The Future of University Education

Ikeda: The announcement in 2006 that the population of Japan has begun to decrease for the first time caused a great stir. In recent years, the number of births in Japan has been falling rapidly. There are now fewer university applicants than places available to them, with the result that we have entered a period in which anyone who applies can get in. Many universities are seriously undertaking reforms in the hope of becoming institutions that can survive this. Though conditions differ from country to country, the challenge of university reform is worldwide. In recent years, Harvard University, where you teach, has been conducting an overall review of its curricula in ways that are attracting attention throughout the field of education.

Cox: Yes, this first such review in about thirty years is a subject of discussion all over the university.

Ikeda: As a leading educator, you have devoted your life to the field. That is why I should like to direct this section of our dialogue to the topic of university education in the twenty-first century.

77

Cox: The future direction of university education, not just in America and Japan, but everywhere, is extremely important to the future of humanity.

Ikeda: The United States is one of the world's educational super-powers. Surveys consistently rank its universities – including Harvard, of course – among the best on Earth. In the second half of the twentieth century, about 50 per cent of Nobel laureates in the natural sciences were scholars from the United States. America originated the graduate school system. In recent years, more and more outstanding young students from many countries, including more and more Asians, desire to study at American universities and graduate schools.

What factors have made this brilliant development possible in American universities?

Cox: People do indeed come from all over the world to American higher-educational institutions such as the Massachusetts Institute of Technology, the California Institute of Technology and Stanford, Michigan, Georgetown and Harvard universities. One of the reasons, surely, is that, after the Second World War, everybody wanted to go somewhere to study in English so they could master the language that has become the lingua franca of the whole world, at least for the time being. This may change. If Chinese someday becomes the leading international language, maybe everybody will want to study in Beijing or Shanghai.

Ikeda: It is estimated that English is spoken by a billion people today, and the number seems likely to grow. With everything from scholarly dissertations to Internet homepages being written in English, the ability to use it is indispensable. The Soka schools and Soka University place great emphasis on teaching English.

Cox: Another aspect of the attraction of American schools is our interesting mixture of educational financing: government, municipal, state and private (including religious). Extensive availability of scholarships gives students the freedom to select their schools. We have a full range of good large, medium and small institutions. However, we have still not solved the problem of how to include young people from poor families.

Ikeda: Its ability to attract large numbers of outstanding students determines how a university develops. Accepting good visiting students from other countries is important because it introduces young people to diverse cultures and values and permits them to form friendships and have experiences they will treasure throughout life.

Many Japanese universities are trying to attract visiting students, but the system of scholarships and the everyday environment are still substandard. Japan has many problems to overcome before it can become an educational superpower.

The Inefficient Lecture System – Students Must Play a Major Role

Cox: Undeniably, attracting students from all over the world has been a major source of the development and vitalization at Harvard.

Ikeda: Soka University of America, a liberal arts college that I founded and that opened in 2001, already has students from more than thirty countries. One of its main characteristics is its concentration on education on human nature, in classes of between ten and twenty students. In addition to hearing lectures, students vitalize and improve their powers of learning by engaging in round-table discussions and conversations with their teachers. Small classes permit faculty members to know their students by name and in person and to employ a warm, face-to-face dialogic method of instruction.

Cox: A lot of the best kind of education is personal interchange among teachers and students. As we know from surveys and studies performed by the Harvard Graduate School of Education and others, the lecture-hall system, in which teachers talk and students listen, is the least effective form of education. In such situations, which are all too common, students retain less of what they hear. They learn far more from working together in small groups or on shared research projects. Interestingly, they even seem to learn more through discussion than they do through attending lectures. In spite of all the evidence, however, people keep lecturing.

Ikeda: Yes. Though long criticized, lecturing is deeply rooted. Over a century ago, Woodrow Wilson, the twenty-eighth president of the United States and a driving force behind the formation of the League of Nations, sharply criticized formal lectures as useless and boring. But still, today, teachers who are unwilling to grow and innovate constantly fall into the same old practice.

Cox: Well, I hope not all lectures are boring! Still, the likelihood that they are is enough to make university professors blush. Professors in higher education are partly responsible. They tend to be rather conservative and set in their ways, especially in relation to the content and method of their teaching.

Ikeda: In Japan, recent years have seen the introduction of a system permitting students to evaluate professors' lectures. They candidly complain that some of them are boring or hard to understand.

In universities, students must always play the main role. Teachers must not be considered superior to them. After all, the students are paying the bills. Sloppiness on the part of faculty members is impermissible. As long as the tendency for the faculty to be careless goes uncorrected, universities cannot survive.

Cox: As much as possible, I try to enlist students in whatever research I'm doing. I always break them up into small, short-term or long-term groups, do a lot of discussion in class, and try to draw them out and have them contribute.

Full-Blooded Dialogue – The Quintessence of Education

Ikeda: That is a splendid system. Your students are very fortunate. To reveal its brilliance, a diamond must be polished. Cultivation and character formation depend on contact with other human beings. Even in intellectual pursuits, we refine ourselves through encounters with different people. What are some of the things you learned from your instructors when you were a student?

Cox: The first thing that comes to mind is enthusiasm. A teacher's enthusiasm and passion for, and involvement in, what he or she is doing communicate at an emotional level. If the professor seems a little bored by his subject, the student will be even more bored.

My major mentor at Harvard, James Luther Adams, was a man of great enthusiasms about the things he studied. I could walk into his office for a talk, and he'd say, 'Oh, look at this book I just got. You must read it. I was up reading it all night!'

Students learn much from human contacts of this kind.

Ikeda: That is very true. In a famous speech delivered at Harvard, Ralph Waldo Emerson, a major figure in the nineteenth-century American renaissance, said that the role of the university is to teach the foundations of learning and to train students. More than this, however, a university must be a place that awakens creativity. It must feed the intellectual flame and ignite the minds of the young people gathered together to learn.

The teacher's mission is to illuminate young people's minds with the light of wisdom and awake the will to study. To do this, the teacher, too, must be alight with enthusiasm for learning. Otherwise, it is impossible to strike sparks in young minds. From my own experience, I can say that a casual word from a teacher can be a source of joy for students. They never forget instruction and discussion provided by teachers outside the classroom.

Cox: I agree. A student chooses to work with a certain teacher out of respect and admiration. It makes a huge difference if that teacher expresses appreciation for anything, small or large, that the student accomplishes.

And another thing: students produce more for teachers who expect more from them. For example, once in a seminar, James Luther Adams asked me to report on an article in a Dutch journal. When I objected that I didn't know Dutch, he said, 'You know German, don't you?' And I admitted I did know – some. Then he said, 'Go to the library and take out a Dutch dictionary and have your report ready next Thursday.' Responding to his expectations of me, I assure you that I learned some Dutch in that one week.

Ikeda: Encouragement and praise help people develop. But doing so requires teachers to respect their students as equal individual human beings and to be affectionately concerned about their cultivation.

Cox: Are you familiar with the work of the educator Paulo Freire (1921–97)?

Ikeda: Yes, I have talked about him with people from Brazilian universities. He was one of the most important Brazilian educators and thinkers of the twentieth century, a man who devoted himself entirely to eradicating illiteracy among the poor. In his major written work *Pedagogy of the Oppressed*, he wrote

82

that education must entail mutual enlightenment and learning by both teacher and student.

Cox: He condemned as mistaken the general educational system, which he described as the 'big jug, little mug' theory. The teacher, who has a big jug of knowledge, pours droplets of it into the student's little mug. He felt this is the wrong way to go about it.

Ikeda: I see. He meant that knowledge should not be imparted in bits and pieces. He argued that education is a dialogue of communications. Instead of being the transmission of knowledge, it is an encounter in which subjects converse mutually.

For the mere transmission of knowledge, studying textbooks is enough. But textbooks do not create highly sensitive, creative human beings. The essence of education is for teachers and students to refine their personalities and seek truth through dialogue. In this way, they attain real learning on a deeper level. This was an article of faith for Tsunesaburo Makiguchi, the originator of the Soka (value-creating) educational philosophy.

Cox: I consider students as team players in a collegial enterprise. I do not merely tell them things. Ultimately, they realize that, as we work together, they are contributing to my own further education, too. And this pleases them.

Compartmentalization of Learning – The Purpose of Knowledge

Ikeda: Over the years, I have talked with many educators. The truly first-rate among them all are happy to admit that teaching deepens their own learning and stimulates their further development.

Now to shift the topic somewhat, I should like to turn to the issue of fragmentation in education. In a message entitled 'The University of the Twenty-First Century – Cradle of World Citizens', which I delivered to the first graduating class of Soka University of America in May 2005, I discussed the damage being done by the specialization and compartmentalization of learning.

The birth and development of the graduate school system have made education and learning more sophisticated and intense. Concomitantly, emphasis has shifted away from all-round human cultivation to research. As early as the beginning of the twentieth century, a certain scholar at Princeton University complained that the number of students and teachers who submerged themselves in research while forgetting to cultivate their humanity was increasing. Speaking of the fragmentation of knowledge, the departmentalization of interests, and the dehumanization of learning, he argued that the totality was being destroyed and learning was being broken into pieces in a process already manifest in the graduate school. This is not a purely American phenomenon but a universal trend.

Cox: Harvard faces the same problem. Departments are isolated in different buildings. Entering a different building is entering a different field of learning. This can be embarrassing. Considerable efforts are being made to facilitate more intra-faculty communication, joint teaching and cooperative teaching. But much remains to be done.

Ikeda: Of course, arranging exchanges between students of different departments scattered over a huge campus is difficult. It is even harder for a university such as Harvard, with facilities spread all over town. Still, on the two occasions on which I have visited Harvard to make speeches, I have observed an impressive extent of open, interdepartmental exchange among faculty members there.

Cox: As you know, our department and the Harvard School of Public Health are in downtown Boston, and the Business School is way across the river. More than a matter of physical distance, this arrangement hampers theoretical consolidation of fields of learning. Division between different faculties is kind of a metaphor for the current fragmentation of knowledge.

Ikeda: The important thing is never to lose sight of the purposes of research and knowledge as we strive to broaden and deepen both. Unfortunately, the more we subdivide and specialize, the more we tend to forget our points of origin. As this happens, learning often comes to exist as an end in itself. In our dialogue, Joseph Rotblat, a scientist who devoted his life to the elimination of nuclear weapons, expressed grave concern on this point: '. . . many scientists feel that the application of their work is none of their business and that they are committed to conduct scientific research for the sake of science . . . I believe that this is an immoral attitude. Yet today, many scientists think this way.'[1] This comment amounts to a summary of Professor Rotblat's legacy.

We need both a consolidated learning that integrates and evaluates segmented knowledge and an ethical philosophy to serve as a foundation. This need is one of the reasons for the recent reconsideration of the liberal arts and their approach to all-round education.

Cox: That is true. Specialization, over-specialization and super-specialization make it very hard to ask fundamental questions about moral purposes. The outcome is that many institutions of higher learning continue to produce people who are very good with facts but lack opportunities to think about values.

Ikeda: The Spanish philosopher José Ortega y Gasset stressed the importance of education as cultivation. In his *Mission of the University*, first published in 1930, he wrote that we have unreasonably expanded specialized education, which in the medieval university was just budding. To this we have added research activities and have almost totally renounced education as cultivation. Today Europe is reaping the result of this patent outrage. The growing numbers of intellectuals oblivious to the philosophical reasons for human life and absorbed entirely in their own special fields vexed him. He called them the new barbarians. His misgivings were realized with the outbreak of the Second World War, in which millions of innocent lives were sacrificed to scientifically developed nuclear and other kinds of weaponry.

Cox: This is a historical lesson that humanity must never forget. I remember once saying to you at Harvard how much we need a place that is nobody's exclusive turf but an open, genuinely welcoming, permanent place where people from different departments and divisions can come together and talk and share a common space.

In 1993, you founded the Boston Research Center for the 21st Century. It is located very near the geographical centre of the university, a few steps from Harvard Yard and less than a block from our Faculty Club. There is no comparable facility anywhere on the Harvard campus. In a sense, the centre makes tremendous contributions to Harvard University as a whole and is likely to continue doing so on an even larger scale in the years to come.

Ikeda: Your generous praise is most encouraging. The cooperation of Harvard has enabled us to hold many different symposia and seminars at the Boston Research Center for the 21st Century. With the attendance of first-class scholars from many fields – including yourself, of course – we have tried to search out solutions to such pressing problems as religious and ethnic strife, poverty and the environment.

Cox: Those conferences were all very good. But the space itself is important; it is beautiful and well kept, which makes a big difference. People often remind me of occurrences there that could have taken place nowhere else. The atmosphere there is unique. We need more places like that.

Creating Value – The Challenge of Religion and Education

Ikeda: The goal of the centre is to promote dialogues between civilizations. Serving as a discussion plaza for large numbers of scholars is consonant with that goal.

Now I should like to discuss the relation between religion and education as a continuation of what we said earlier about intellectual fragmentation. Today, as science forges ahead, religion tends to take a kind of backseat as unscientific and irrational. Unfortunately, throughout history, raging religious fanatics have done great damage. But, on the positive side, religion has provided indispensable models for living in a better fashion. If religion is renounced by an age that believes exclusively in science, conscience and morality will be marginalized. Then arrogance will return in disastrous ways.

Cox: I don't accept the idea that, as science advances, there's a smaller and smaller place for religion. Religion is about meaning, values and community. None of these things can be understood or fully explained by the unaided scientific method. Nor can science answer the basic question of why there is a world anyway.

As long as we are human, we ask why we are here and what part we play in the whole. These are the questions that religions have addressed for centuries and centuries. When we stop asking such questions, we stop being human and set out on the road to becoming robots.

Ikeda: I agree. Science can explain how human beings are born but is incapable of answering fundamental questions such as why we were born at all, why in a specific era or country, and how we should live our lives.

My friend Dr M. S. Swaminathan, president of the Pugwash Conferences on Science and World Affairs, devoted himself to improving strains of wheat and rice in ways that contributed to averting famine in India and the whole of Asia. The need to know why people in his homeland were starving and how to save them inspired him to study agricultural science. I consistently tell students at Soka University and the Soka schools to have a good grasp on the reasons for study and learning.

Cox: Yes, especially in our time, a sense of mission and purpose requires us to know the reasons for learning and research.

Ikeda: Life is too complex to be completely explained in terms of science alone. As long as we are alive, we will confront contradictions and hardships. Buddhism and other religions exist to provide answers to the suffering of humanity. They direct us to the path towards overcoming difficulties and striving for higher goals and ideals. True religion and science do not oppose each other. As my mentor Josei Toda often said, the more science progresses, the more it validates Buddhism.

Cox: As I understand it, the primary goal of Soka Gakkai is to create value. That is very important. We talk a lot about values in education and moral reasoning and so on, but the actual creation of value, rather than the mere replication of the already existing ones, is what we must do. History moves on. New challenges arise. Therefore we need new value insights. An education that simply perpetuates the status quo is of limited usefulness. Encouraging people – almost pushing them – into creativity is necessary. In this sense, Tsunesaburo Makiguchi was a true educational reformer.

Ikeda: He was a great educator who developed a living pedagogy based on his own on-the-spot experience as a primary-school principal. Putting children's happiness first, he refused to ingratiate himself with people in power, and thus incurred their disapproval. He was frequently forced to change schools and submitted to other harassment. Contact with the Buddhism of Nichiren caused him to advance from his starting point as an educational reformer to become a religious reformer, striving to bring about fundamental improvement in human beings. In the teachings of Nichiren Buddhism, he discovered how to create supreme values and how to live in the most value-creative way possible.

As heir to the ideals of Tsunesaburo Makiguchi and Josei Toda, I have established value-creating educational facilities in many parts of the world on all levels ranging from kindergarten to university graduate schools. Our graduates are now doing brilliant work for peace and humanity all over the planet. For me, this is a source of unparalleled happiness.

Cox: I will take great pleasure in seeing how the Soka schools and Soka University in Japan and Soka University of America progress.

Ikeda: I hope that you will continue to do so and will advise the faculty and student body of Soka University of America on various matters. Keeping in mind Josei Toda's admonition to struggle today for the sake of people who will live 200 years from now, I dedicate myself completely to education, which I consider my major work.

Now, as we conclude, please allow me to thank you for taking a great deal of your time to share this dialogue with me. The chance to discuss important matters with one of the leading religious leaders, educators and theologians in the United States has been highly instructive and fruitful.

Cox: It is I who should thank you for this very enjoyable discussion. I have learned a great deal and absorbed much that is new to me. This kind of dialogue uncovers new and unfamiliar insights and possibilities. Because he knew this, Socrates used dialogue as his basic teaching method.

Ikeda: I am grateful for all the lessons you have taught me. As Socrates said, 'An unexamined life is not worth living,'[2] and 'the really important thing is not to live, but to live well.'[3] My own conviction is that, as long as we live, we must move forward, always creating new values.

APPENDIX 1

Mahayana Buddhism and Twenty-First-Century Civilization

A speech delivered by Daisaku Ikeda at Harvard University, Cambridge, Massachusetts, 24 September 1993

Nothing could please me more than to be back at Harvard University, to speak with faculty and students at this time-honoured institution of unexcelled academic endeavour. To Professor Nur Yalman, Professor Harvey Cox, Professor John Kenneth Galbraith and all the others who have made my visit possible, I extend my thanks.

The Continuity of Life and Death

It was the Greek philosopher Heraclitus who declared that all things are in a state of flux and that change is the essential nature of reality. Indeed, everything, whether it lies in the realm of natural phenomena or of human affairs, changes continuously. Nothing maintains exactly the same state for even the briefest instant; the most solid-seeming rocks and minerals are subject to the erosive effects of time. But during this century of war and revolution, normal change and flux seem to have been accelerated and magnified. We have seen the most extraordinary panorama of social transformations.

The Buddhist term for the ephemeral aspect of reality is 'the transience of all phenomena' (*shogyō mujō*, in Japanese). In the Buddhist cosmology, this concept is described as the repeated cycles of formation, continuance, decline and disintegration through which all systems must pass. During our lives as human beings, we experience transience as the four sufferings; the suffering of birth (and of day-to-day existence), that of illness, of ageing and, finally, of death. No human being is exempt from these sources of pain. It was, in fact, human distress, in particular the problem of death, that spawned the formation of religious and philosophical systems. It is said that Shakyamuni was inspired to seek the truth by his accidental encounters with many sorrows at the gates of the palace in which he was raised. Plato stated that true philosophers are always engaged in the practice of dying, while Nichiren, founder of the school of Buddhism followed by members of Soka Gakkai International, admonishes us to 'first of all learn about death, and then about other things'.[1]

Death weighs heavily on the human heart as an inescapable reminder of the finite nature of our existence. However seemingly limitless the wealth or power we might attain, the reality of our eventual demise cannot be avoided. From ancient times, humanity has sought to conquer the fear and apprehension surrounding death by finding ways in which to partake of the eternal. Through this quest, people have learned to overcome control by instinctual modes of survival and have developed the characteristics that we recognize as uniquely human. In that perspective, we can see why the history of religion coincides with the history of humankind.

Modern civilization has attempted to ignore death. We have diverted our gaze from this most fundamental of concerns as we try to drive death into the shadows. For many people living today, death is the mere absence of life; it is blankness, it is the void. Life is identified with all that is good: with being, rationality and light. In contrast, death is perceived as evil, as nothingness and as the dark and irrational. Only the negative perception of death prevails.

We cannot, however, ignore death, and the attempt to do so has exacted a heavy price. The horrific and ironic climax of modern civilization has been in our time what Zbigniew Brzezinski has called the 'century of megadeath'. Today, a wide range of issues is now forcing a re-examination and re-evaluation of the significance of death. They include questions about brain death and death with dignity, the function of hospices, alternative funerary styles and rites and research into death and dying by writers such as Elizabeth Kubler-Ross.

We finally seem to be ready to recognize the fundamental error in our view of life and death. We are beginning to understand that death is more than the absence of life; that death, together with active life, is necessary for the formation of a larger, more essential, whole. This greater whole reflects the deeper continuity of life and death that we experience as individuals and express as culture. A central challenge for the coming century will be to establish a culture based on an understanding of the relationship of life and death and of life's essential eternity. Such an attitude does not disown death, but directly confronts and correctly positions it within the larger context of life.

Buddhism speaks of an intrinsic nature (*hosshō* in Japanese, sometimes translated as 'Dharma nature') existing within the depths of phenomenal reality. This nature depends upon and responds to environmental conditions, and it alternates between states of emergence and latency. All phenomena, including life and death, can be seen as elements within the cycle of emergence and latency, or manifestation and withdrawal.

Cycles of life and death can be likened to the alternating periods of sleep and wakefulness. Just as sleep prepares us for the next day's activity, death can be seen as a state in which we rest and replenish ourselves for new life. In this light, death should be acknowledged, along with life, as a blessing to be appreciated. The Lotus Sutra, the core of Mahayana Buddhism, states that the purpose of existence, the eternal cycles of life and death, is to be 'happy and at ease'. It further teaches that sustained faith and practice enable us to know a deep and abiding joy in death as well as in life, to be equally 'happy and at ease'[2] with both. Nichiren describes the attainment of this state as the 'greatest of all joys'.[3]

If the tragedies of this century of war and revolution have taught us anything, it is the folly of believing that reform of external factors, such as social systems, is the linchpin to achieving happiness. I am convinced that in the coming century, the greatest emphasis must be placed on fostering change that is directed inwards. In addition, our efforts must be inspired by a new understanding of life and death.

There are three broad areas where Mahayana Buddhism can help solve the problems suggested above, and make a positive difference to civilization in the twenty-first century. Let us consider those aspects of Buddhism that offer workable, constructive guidance.

The Buddhist Emphasis on Dialogue

Since its inception, the philosophy of Buddhism has been associated with peace and pacifism. That emphasis derives principally from the consistent rejection of violence combined with stress on dialogue and discussion as the best means of resolving conflict. Descriptions of the life of Shakyamuni provide a good illustration. His life was completely uninfluenced by dogma, and his interactions with his fellows stressed the importance of dialogue. The sutra recounting the travels that culminated his Buddhist practice begins with an episode in which the aged Shakyamuni uses the power of language to avert an invasion.[4]

According to the sutra, Shakyamuni, then eighty years old, did not directly admonish the minister of Magadha, a large country bent on conquering the neighbouring state of Vajji. Instead, he spoke persuasively about the principles by which nations prosper and decline. His discourse dissuaded the minister from implementing the planned attack. The final chapter of the same sutra concludes with a moving description of Shakyamuni on his deathbed. As he lay dying, he repeatedly urged his disciples to raise any uncertainties that they might have about the Buddhist law (Dharma) or its practice, so that they would not find themselves regretting unasked questions after his passing. Up until his final moment, Shakyamuni actively sought out dialogue, and the drama of his final voyage from beginning to end is illuminated by the light of language, skilfully wielded by one who was truly a 'master of words'.

Why was Shakyamuni able to employ language with such freedom and to such effect? What made him such a peerless master of dialogue? I believe that his fluency was due to the expansiveness of his enlightened state, utterly free of all dogma, prejudice and attachment. The following quotation is illustrative: 'I perceived a single, invisible arrow piercing the hearts of the people.'[5] The 'arrow' symbolizes a prejudicial mindset, an unreasoning emphasis on individual differences. At that time India was going through transition and upheaval, and the horrors of conflict and war were an ever-present reality. To Shakyamuni's penetrating gaze, it was clear that the underlying cause of the conflict was attachment to distinctions, to ethnic, national and other differences.

In the early years of this century, Josiah Royce (one of many important philosophers Harvard University has given the world) declared that: 'Reform, in such matters, must come, if at all, from within . . . The public as a whole is whatever the processes that occur, for good or evil, in individual minds, may determine.'[6]

As Royce points out, the 'invisible arrow' of evil is not to be found in the existence of races and classes external to ourselves, but is embedded in our own hearts. The conquest of our own prejudicial thinking, our own attachment to difference, is the necessary precondition for open dialogue. Such discussion, in turn, is essential for the establishment of peace and universal respect for human rights. It was his own complete absence of prejudice that enabled Shakyamuni to expound the law with such freedom, adapting his style of teaching to the character and capacity of the person to whom he was speaking.

Whether he was mediating a communal dispute over water rights, converting a violent criminal or admonishing someone who objected to the practice of begging, Shakyamuni attempted first to make others aware of the 'arrow' of their inner evil. The power of his extraordinary character brought these words to the lips of one contemporaneous sovereign: 'Those whom we, with weapons, cannot force to surrender, you subdue unarmed.'[7]

Only by overcoming attachment to differences can a religion rise above an essentially tribal outlook to offer a global faith. Nichiren, for example, dismissed the shogunal authorities who were persecuting him, as the 'rulers of this little island country'.[8] His vision was broader, directed towards establishing a religious spirit that would embody universal values and transcend the confines of a single state.

Dialogue is not limited to formal debate or placid exchange that wafts by like a spring breeze. There are times when, to break the grip of arrogance, speech must be like the breath of fire. Thus, although we typically associate Shakyamuni and Nāgārjuna only with mildness, it was the occasional ferocity of their speech that earned them the sobriquet of 'those who deny everything'[9] in their respective eras.

Similarly, Nichiren, who demonstrated a familial affection and tender concern for the common people, was uncompromising in his confrontations with corrupt and degenerate authority. Always unarmed in the chronically violent Japan of his time, he relied exclusively and unflinchingly on the power of persuasion and non-violence. He was tempted with the promise of absolute power if he renounced his faith, and threatened with the beheading of his parents if he adhered to his beliefs. Nevertheless, he maintained the courage of his convictions. The following passage, written upon his exile to a distant island from which no one were expected to return, typifies his leonine tone: 'Whatever obstacles I might encounter, so long as persons of wisdom do not prove my teachings to be false, I will never yield!'[10]

Nichiren's faith in the power of language was absolute. If more people were to pursue dialogue in an equally unrelenting manner, the inevitable conflicts of human life would surely find easier resolution. Prejudice would yield to empathy and war would give way to peace. Genuine dialogue results in the transformation of opposing viewpoints, changing them from wedges that drive people apart into bridges that link them together.

During the Second World War, Soka Gakkai, an organization based on the teachings of Nichiren, challenged head-on the forces of Japanese militarism. As a result, many members were imprisoned, beginning with the founder and first president Tsunesaburo Makiguchi. Far from recanting, Makiguchi continued to explain to his guards and interrogators the principles of Buddhism. They were the very ideas that had made him a 'thought criminal' in the first place. He died at the age of seventy-three, still in confinement.

Josei Toda was heir to the spiritual legacy of Makiguchi, and he became the second president of the organization. He emerged from the ordeal of two years' imprisonment declaring his faith in the unity of the global human family. He then preached widely among the population, who were lost and suffering in the aftermath of the war. Toda also bequeathed to us, his youthful disciples, the mission of building a world free of nuclear weapons.

With this as our historical and philosophical basis, Soka Gakkai International remains committed to the role of dialogue in the advancement of peace, education and culture. At present, we are engaged in forging bonds of solidarity with citizens in 115 [192, as of July 2009] countries and regions around the world. For my own part, I wish only to continue my efforts to speak with people all over the Earth in order to contribute in some small way to the greater happiness of humankind.

Restoring Humanity

What role can Buddhism play in the restoration and rejuvenation of humanity? In an age marked by widespread religious revival, we need always to ask: Does religion make people stronger, or weaker? Does it encourage what is good or what is evil in them? Are they made better and wiser by religion? While the authority of Marx as social prophet has been largely undermined by the collapse of socialism in Eastern Europe and the former Soviet Union, there is an important truth contained in his description of religion as the 'opiate of the masses'. In fact, there is reason for concern that more than a few of the religions finding new life in the twilight of this century are characterized by dogmatism and insularity, traits that run counter to the accelerating trend towards interdependence and cross-cultural interaction.

With this in mind, let us examine the relative weight that different belief systems assign to self-reliance, as opposed to dependence on powers external to the self. These two tendencies correspond roughly to the Christian concepts of free will and grace. Broadly speaking, the passage from medieval to modern Europe coincided with a steady movement away from a theistic determinism, towards ever-greater emphasis on free will and human responsibility. Human abilities were encouraged, and reliance on external, abstract authority declined, making way for the great achievements of science and technology. More and more people began to believe in the omnipotence of reason and its scientific fruits. But to be blindly convinced of the power of technology can lead to the hubris of assuming that there is nothing we are unable to accomplish. It may be true that dependence on some external authority led people to underestimate both our potential and our responsibility, but excessive faith in our own powers is not the answer; it has, in fact, produced a dangerous overconfidence in ourselves.

We are now seeking a third path, a new balance between faith in ourselves and recognition of a power that is greater than we are. These words of Nichiren illustrate the subtle and richly suggestive Mahayana perspective on attaining enlightenment: 'People are certainly self-empowered, and yet they are not self-empowered . . . people are certainly other-empowered, and yet they are not other-empowered.'[11] The persuasive argument of Buddhism is its conviction that the greatest good is derived from the dynamic fusion and balancing of internal and external forces.

Similarly, John Dewey, in *A Common Faith*, asserts that it is 'the religious', rather than specific religions, that is of vital importance. While religions all too quickly fall into dogmatism and fanaticism, 'that which is religious' has the power to 'unify interests and energies' and to 'direct action and generate the heat of emotion and the light of intelligence'. Likewise, 'the religious' enables the realization of those benefits that Dewey identifies as 'the values of art in all its forms, of knowledge, of effort, and of rest after striving, of education and fellowship, of friendship and love, of growth in mind and body'.[12] Dewey does not identify a specific external power. For him 'the religious' is a generalized term for that which supports and encourages people in the active pursuit of the good and the valuable. 'The religious', as he defines it, helps those who help themselves.

As Dewey understood, and as the sad outcome of people's self-worship in modern times has demonstrated, without assistance we are incapable of living up to our potential. Only by relying on and merging with the external can we fully activate all our capabilities. Thus, we need help, but our human potential does not come from outside; it is, and always has been, of us and within us. How any given religious tradition handles the balance between interior and exterior forces will, I believe, decisively affect its long-term viability. Anyone involved in religion must constantly work on keeping the balance, if we do not want to repeat history. For if we are not attentive, religion can enslave us to dogma and to its own authority just as easily as the religious impulse can serve as a vehicle for restoration and rejuvenation.

Perhaps because our Buddhist movement is so human centred, Harvey Cox of the Harvard Divinity School has described it as an effort to define the humanistic direction of religion. Indeed, Buddhism is not merely a theoretical construct; it helps us to steer our lives, as we actually live them, moment by moment, towards the achievement of happiness and worth. Thus, Nichiren states: 'If in a single moment of life we exhaust the pains and trials of millions of *kalpas*, then instant after instant there will arise in us the three Buddha bodies with which we are eternally endowed.'[13] The expression 'we exhaust the pains and trials of millions of *kalpas*' refers to the ability to confront each of life's problems with our full being, awakening the entire consciousness, leaving no inner resource untapped. By wholeheartedly and directly meeting the challenges of life, we bring forth from within ourselves 'the three Buddha bodies with which we are eternally endowed'. It is the light of this internal wisdom that constantly encourages and guides us towards true and correct action.

The vibrant tones of the drums, horns and other musical instruments that appear throughout the Lotus Sutra work metaphorically to encourage the human will to live. The function of the Buddha nature is always to urge us to be strong, good, and wise. The message of the sutra is one of human restoration.

The Interrelationship of All Things

Buddhism provides a philosophical basis for the symbiotic co-existence of all things. Among the many images in the Lotus Sutra, a particularly compelling one is the merciful rain that falls everywhere, equally, moistening the vast expanse of the earth and bringing forth new life from all the trees and grasses, large and small. This scene, depicted with the vividness, grandeur and beauty characteristic of the Lotus Sutra, symbolizes the enlightenment of all people touched by the Buddha's law. At the same time, it is a magnificent tribute to the rich diversity of human and all other forms of sentient and non-sentient life. Thus, each living thing manifests the enlightenment of which it is capable; each contributes to the harmony of the grand concert of symbiosis. In Buddhist terminology, 'dependent origination' (*engi*) describes these relationships. Nothing and nobody exists in isolation. Each individual being functions to create the environment that sustains all other existences. All things are mutually supporting and interrelated, forming a living cosmos – what modern philosophy might term a semantic whole. That is the conceptual framework through which Mahayana Buddhism views the natural universe.

Speaking through *Faust*, Goethe gives voice to a similar vision: 'Into the whole, how all things blend, each in the other working, living.'[14] These lines are striking for their remarkable affinity with Buddhist thought. Although Johann Peter Eckermann criticized Goethe for 'lacking confirmation of his presentiments',[15] the intervening years have seen a steadily swelling affirmation of the deductive vision in both Goethe and Buddhist thought.

Consider, for example, the concept of causation. When viewed in terms of dependent origination, causal relationships differ fundamentally from the mechanistic idea of cause and effect that, according to modern science, holds sway over the objective natural world. In the scientific model, reality is divorced from subjective human concerns. When an accident or disaster takes place, for example, a mechanistic theory of causation can be used to pursue and identify how the accident occurred. It is silent, however, on other points, including the question of why certain individuals and not others should find themselves caught up in the tragic event. Indeed, the mechanistic view of nature requires the deliberate dismissal of existential questions.

In contrast, the Buddhist understanding of causation is more broadly defined and takes account of human existence. It seeks to directly address these poignant uncertainties, as in the following exchange that occurred early in Shakyamuni's career: 'What is the cause of ageing and death? Birth is the cause of ageing and death.'[16]

In a later era, through a process of exhaustive personal inquiry, Zhiyi, the founder of the Chinese Tiantai school of Buddhism, developed a theoretical structure that included such concepts as the 'three thousand realms in a single moment of life'. It is not only sweeping in scope and rigorous in elaboration, but is entirely compatible with modern science. While limitations of time prohibit discussion of his system, it is worth mentioning that many contemporary fields of inquiry – for example, ecology, transpersonal psychology and quantum mechanics – have interesting points in common with Buddhism in their approach and conclusions.

The Buddhist emphasis on relatedness and interdependence may seem to suggest that individual identity is obscured. Buddhist scripture addresses this in the following passage: 'You are your own master. Could anyone else be your master? When you have gained control over yourself, you have found a master of rare value.'[17] A second passage reads: 'Be lamps unto yourselves. Rely on yourselves. Hold fast to the Law as a lamp, do not rely on anything else.'[18] Both passages urge us to live independently, true to ourselves and unswayed by others. The 'self' referred to here, however, is not the Buddhist 'lesser self' (shōga), caught up in the snares of egoism. Rather, it is the 'greater self' (taiga), fused with the life of the universe through which cause and effect intertwine over the infinite reaches of space and time.

The greater, cosmic self is related to the unifying and integrating 'self' that Jung perceived in the depths of the ego. It is also similar to Ralph Waldo Emerson's 'The universal beauty, to which every part and particle is equally related; the eternal One'.[19]

I am firmly convinced that a large-scale awakening to the greater self will lead to a world of creative co-existence in the coming century. Recall the lines of Walt Whitman, in which he sings the praises of the human spirit:

But that I, turning to thee O soul, thou actual Me,
And lo, thou gently masterest the orbs,
Thou matest Time, smilest content at Death,
And fillest, swellest full the vastness of space.[20]

The 'greater self' of Mahayana Buddhism is another way of expressing the openness and expansiveness of character that embraces the sufferings of all people as one's own. This 'self' always seeks ways of alleviating the pain and augmenting the happiness of others, here, amid the realities of everyday life. Only the solidarity brought about by such natural human nobility will break down the isolation of the modern 'self' and lead to the dawning of new hope for civilization. Furthermore, it is the dynamic, vital awakening of the greater self that will enable each of us, as individuals, to experience both life and death with equal delight. Thus, as Nichiren stated: 'We use the aspects of birth, ageing, sickness and death to adorn the tower that is our body.'[21]

It is my earnest desire and prayer that in the twenty-first century each member of the human family will let shine the natural lustre of this inner 'treasure tower.' Filling our azure planet with the chorus of open dialogue, humankind will move on into the new millennium.

APPENDIX 2

Religion, Values and Politics in a Religiously Pluralistic World

_____

The McGill Lecture on religious dialogue delivered by Professor Harvey Cox in Montreal, September 2006

We live at a time of curious paradox in the relations of religious traditions to each other. On the one hand there are more organizations, conferences and seminars devoted to inter-religious dialogue than at any time in previous history. This historic gathering in Montreal is an exciting example, but such events are happening all over the world. As we meet here another significant conference is going on in Morocco. However, we also live in an era of dangerous animosity between and among religious traditions. Hindus and Muslims still distrust each other on the Indian subcontinent. Jews and Muslims have exacerbated the rivalries in Israel/Palestine. Professor Samuel Huntington warns that we may be headed for a bloody 'clash of civilizations' between what he designates as the 'Islamic' and the 'Judaeo-Christian' civilizations.

Maybe these two contradictory trends have a common explanation: we can no longer avoid each other. There was a time when the vast majority of adherents of any tradition (with the possible exception of Jews) could live their whole lives in blissful ignorance even of the existence of other faiths. Now all that is changed. Due to tides of immigration, travel, the Internet, films and the diaspora of religions all over the globe, we are – for bane or for blessing – now all each other's neighbours.

All this is well known, so I would like to direct my remarks here to three angles of a triangle that complicates what I prefer to call 'religious peacemaking' rather than merely dialogue.

- The first is the intensely *political context* within which the interaction among religious traditions has always gone on and within which religious peacemaking must proceed today.
- The second is the appearance in the last century, in each of the traditions, of what some refer to as a *'fundamentalist' wing*, a strong reaction against interfaith dialogues as a lethal danger to the integrity of the faith itself.
- The third is a certain lack of *candour* or polite reticence that sometimes inadvertently hampers the interfaith element of communication and religious peacemaking.

I would like to speak about the second of these challenges first, and then circle back to the other two.

Circling the Wagons

The term 'fundamentalist' first was coined in the early twentieth century to designate a specific movement in American Protestantism whose leaders complained that such ideas as biblical criticism, evolution and the social gospel were undermining the indispensable 'fundamentals' of Christianity. They insisted on fidelity to the virgin birth, the verbal inspiration of scripture, the substitutionary atonement and the physical resurrection, without which, they claimed, one could not call what was left 'Christianity' at all.

In the years since then, however, the term 'fundamentalism' has been applied almost indiscriminately across the board to different traditions, sometimes helpfully and sometimes in a confusing manner. Muslims do not appreciate the term being applied to them. Nor do even the most conservative Jews. The term hardly clarifies the ultra-conservative movements in Hinduism, Buddhism or Shinto. Nevertheless, I will use the term here to designate the highly conservative wings appearing in each of the traditions. They do have some common qualities. They each selectively retrieve elements from their own traditions and deploy them on two fronts. On one front they oppose certain elements of the 'modern' world (usually including the equality of women) while, however, embracing others (such as modern communications technologies). On the other front, and usually much more vigorously, they oppose those sectors in their own traditions that accept some qualities of modernity that they do not. In fact 'fundamentalists' almost always direct their bitterest barrages not at the outsiders, but at the traitors within the camp. We can see examples of this 'second front' on which fundamentalists fight (which is really often the primary front) everywhere we look.

The Muslim Brotherhood, founded in Egypt, one of whose earliest leaders was Sayyed Qut'b, opposed communism, capitalism and nationalism in the interest of restoring the Muslim *umma* and Koranic justice and equality. But its main attacks were focused on 'pseudo-Muslims' who, its leaders contended, were betraying Islam by using it as a political prop for Western modernist programmes, and thus creating a new era of *'jahila'*, the morass of chaos, impiety and injustice that proceeded the Koran. The enemy that al-Qaeda's leaders have sworn to destroy is not primarily the West, but the allegedly Muslim regimes that tyrannize their own people. They are especially opposed to Saudi Arabia because the regime there rules explicitly in the name of Islam. They strike out against the West not because they 'hate our way of life' but because the West supports the 'pseudo-Muslim' regimes they detest.

In Israel things are not better. This confrontation is sometimes depicted as a battle between religious and secular Israeli Jews. But it is really an internal Jewish struggle between a form of Zionism dating back to Ben Gurion, marked by a mixture of *realpolitik* and selectively retrieved religious motifs ('Zionism' is itself derived from the biblical name of Jerusalem), and an ardent, Messianic Zionism, sparked by the theology of Rabbi Kook and Israel's victory in the 1967 war, a theology that now inspires the West Bank settler movement to 'conquer and settle' the whole of *eretz Israel*, and never, ever return even one square metre.

Likewise the spokesmen of the American religious right, although they attack what they call the 'liberal media', Hollywood, 'activist judges' and stem-cell research, reserve their most potent fusillades for other Christians who disagree with them on these or a host of other issues. Let me point out in passing, however, that the questions that concern them most are not now – as they once were – biblical inerrancy or the doctrine of the atonement but what they call 'social issues', matters within the realm of politics and culture.

The passions enflamed by these struggles all too often lead to violence. The American Christian convicted of killing staff members at a clinic that provided abortions never repented because he believed he was obeying God's word and saving innocent lives. Prime Minister Rabin was assassinated not by a Palestinian but by a devoted messianic Jew acting on what he believed the Torah instructed him to do, preventing the surrender of land that God had given to the Jewish people and saving Jewish lives. Gandhi was not killed by a Muslim, but by a fellow Hindu. Islamist militants direct the majority of their attacks against fellow Muslims, and secondarily against non-Muslims who are supporting them.

In one tradition after another, and everywhere in the world, we can observe this burgeoning of a 'circle-the-wagons' wing, a deepening preoccupation with political/cultural questions, and at times a willingness to resort to violence. Where does this leave the interfaith dialogue?

To put it most bluntly, in my view, most interfaith dialogues – although there are important exceptions – are content to stay with the less difficult elements of the conversations. Most Christians who engage in dialogue strongly prefer to converse with sympathetic Jews, Muslims, Hindus and Buddhists. They rarely try to communicate with the most conservative wings in their own traditions. This is understandable. What dialogically oriented Christian would not rather spend an afternoon with the Dalai Lama than with Gerry Falwell? Of course, in conversations between and among people from different traditions differences always come up, but there is a difference in the differences. They seem to be at a safe remove since they are not a part of my own faith, and are either easily handled or postponed for later.

Candour in Interfaith Conversation

In some interfaith dialogue settings a tacit taboo usually sets in against discussing 'politics', questions that seem disruptive, irrelevant or a threat to the atmosphere of congeniality and collegiality that such meetings are thought to require. At least in the USA, interfaith groups usually avoid any mention of the Israel–Palestine conflict, and it is frowned upon to bring up either 9/11 or the America invasion of Iraq in talks with Muslims. We would prefer to rehearse once more how Jewish Jesus was and what a prominent place he has in the Koran, or muse about how much we have to learn from Buddhist tolerance or Hindu inclusivism. At a time when all our traditions have become so enmeshed in political/cultural turmoil, however, this pattern of tactical avoidance – although it may preserve a feel-good atmosphere – merely succeeds in evading the hardest questions. But it also obscures the inconvenient fact that throughout history the conflicts within and between religious traditions have always been suffused with political elements. Such decontextualized conversations (and I repeat that not all conversations fall into this trap) can therefore lead to a false sense of optimism about interfaith relationships and the inevitable disillusionment that sets in when damaging tensions re-emerge.

The Politics of Religious Peacemaking

It is becoming clear that religious peacemaking is summoned to three interrelated encounters: (1) with other faith traditions; (2) with the 'other wing' in our own tradition; and (3) with the political world within which these first two inevitably take place. To respond to this summons I would like to suggest two changes in the current strategies for religious peacemaking. Let us call them *inter*faith candour and *intra*-faith conversation. Both, as we shall see, will have to proceed within the heavily politicized atmosphere in which all religions live today. This context forms the third side of our triangle, which both the other sides (as with all triangles) join.

The first encounter, *inter*faith candour, would require us to move away from an exclusive emphasis on cultivating harmony and good feelings, and into a phase of honestly questioning the toxic ingredients in both our own and other traditions. We all have them. They leap out of the pages of the scriptures. They blemish the historical records of each of the faiths. Any reader of the Hebrew scriptures, the book of Revelation in the New Testament or the Koran cannot help noticing the blood-stained verses, the so-called 'texts of terror'. We seem very adept at uncovering them in the scriptures of other traditions, less aware of the ones in our own. Also, Jews, Christians and Muslims all have those gory pages in our histories – the conquest of Canaan that was not to spare even children or animals, the Inquisition and First Crusade's loosing of a river of blood in Jerusalem (and the Fourth Crusade's pillaging of Constantinople, one of the most odious *intra*-faith crimes in history) and the sacred texts and prayers the 9/11 hijackers were instructed to read before plunging their planes into buildings. These accounts embarrass us when we read them, and we would sometimes like to forget they are there. But they are there, and we need to help each other – across religious lines – to cope with the vexed question of why they often remain comatose for long periods of time, only to be fanned into flame in order to incite violence at other times.

The question I am raising is both hermeneutical (about how texts are to be interpreted) and political (why and how the context of such interpretations is so critical). I suggest that it is an issue that all faiths must not only grapple with separately, but also that we need to do so together. Since we are all afflicted with the virus, we need to help each other. Also we may be able to examine the texts of other faiths with which we have less immediate emotional involvement or habituated familiarity. Most importantly, however, representatives of one tradition will only be emboldened to engage in such a risky enterprise, with the vulnerabilities it inevitably exposes, if they can be assured that their colleagues in other traditions are taking the same chances. If we can move beyond constantly quoting the exhortations to peacemaking in the Hebrew scriptures, Jesus' commandment to love our neighbours and the Koran's endorsement of religious pluralism to the hard-edged and troublesome texts we all have, it will be – though difficult – a vital service to everyone.

The second encounter, *intra*-faith conversation, suggests that we need to devote much effort to meet, understand, appreciate and argue with the circle-the-wagons wing in each of our traditions. Unless we do, we face the grim prospect of a future in which open-minded members in each faith devote an increasing amount of time to dialogues and colloquies with similarly open-minded members of other faiths, while the ultra-conservative wings in each become more isolated and truculent. We will end up with more and deeper divisions than we once had, only running along internal rather than external fault lines. Ironically, the *inter*faith movement would then be defeated by its own success.

I recognize the serious objection that is immediately raised to such a suggestion: 'You just can't talk to those people.' Fundamentalists, it is said, are against dialogue as a central tenet of faith, while dialoguers affirm it as a central tenet of theirs. Therefore no communication is possible. But the symmetry of this picture does not fully correspond to reality. One of the reasons ultra-conservatives are reluctant to talk with those on the other end of their own tradition's spectrum is that they often feel, sometimes with reason, that the 'liberals' view them with condescension and disrespect. In my country they are often treated dismissively as hicks and rednecks, ignorant and out of step. These stereotypes often make it difficult for them to engage in conversation. But the fact that such *intra*-faith converse can be very difficult is no reason to avoid it. On the contrary, it signals a good reason to try to engage in it.

At Harvard Divinity School we are proud to have been pioneers in *inter*faith dialogue. Our Center for the Study of World Religions, founded in 1958, is the first such centre in a Christian school of theology in America. But for some years now there has been a growing realization that *intra*-faith dialogue is also critically important. Some years ago we invited Rev. Gerry Falwell and some representatives of Liberty University, the institution he founded in Lynchburg, Virginia for a visit. Falwell enthusiastically styles himself a 'fundamentalist', and describes his theology and political stance as 'as conservative as you can get'. Some faculty and students strenuously opposed having him on the campus, and his visit was indeed a tumultuous event. But after his lecture, the highly thoughtful and critical responses given to it, and the challenging questions from the audience, no one thought the visit should not have happened. A few years later, we entertained a group of faculty members from Regent University, founded by Pat Robertson. Their visit included a private conversation with members of our faculty – on how to make Christian values relevant in the public arena – and a well-attended public forum that filled the largest lecture hall in the Divinity School. Although neither visit created any dramatic breakthroughs, they demonstrated that the idea that 'you just can't talk to those people' was not necessarily true.

Intra-faith dialogue is often more difficult than *inter*faith dialogue. Both sides understandably tend to avoid it, albeit for different reasons. But the result is that tensions between the wings within each tradition deepen, and instead of communication we find confrontation, calumny, condemnation and constant threat of schism. As conditions worsen we feel ever-more uncomfortable talking with co-religionists who – many of us believe – are distorting and even demeaning the faith we both share. Sibling rivalry is often the nastiest kind, in the first murder it was brother who killed his own brother – strikingly, over the proper way to sacrifice to the God they both worshipped.

The possibilities for such *intra*-faith dialogue are not, however, as foreboding as they sometimes appear. Here I must speak mainly about the situation I know best, that in my own country. The fact is that the conservative-evangelical-fundamentalist community is neither monolithic nor immobile. It is divided and subdivided along theological, racial, gender, geographical, denominational and political lines. These divisions often collide and conflict, and the internal rhetoric generated is frequently more intense than that which they direct towards their external opponents. Indeed the tone of this internal debate has become even sharper since the American evangelicals who once claimed to have had a decisive role in electing George Bush, are now embracing a wider variety of political and social causes. 'Religious conservative' is no longer identical with 'religious right'.

The splits within the conservative religious community claimed widespread attention in February 2005 when Robert Wenzl, the vice president of the National Association of Evangelicals (NAE), blasted his fellow evangelicals for having 'lost their perspective'. Reaching back into history, he condemned Gerry Falwell's Moral Majority, which had been so active in the 1980s, as 'an aberration and a regrettable one at that' because it was 'flawed by a fatal hubris'. He intimated that the same flaw might still be present in the growing 'mega-churches', so comfortably ensconced in the suburbs rather than in urban areas where the need for justice ministries is so evident. If a spokesman of the National Council of Churches had made such a statement it would have gone unnoticed. But this was a high officer in the NAE, and the headline in the *Boston Globe* reporting his speech carried the headline, 'Official Chides Christian Right.' The following year, Rick Warren, pastor of the huge Saddleback Church in California, led efforts by evangelicals to join other Christians and people of other faiths in the struggle against global warming and against torture.

At the theological level, there is a new atmosphere among American evangelicals. They are openly debating matters that once appeared closed, such as the nature of biblical authority and the possibility of God's redemptive presence in other religions. A heated dispute has also broken out about the eschatology, the theological doctrine of the 'last things', and how the world will end. The argument centres on the vastly popular *Left Behind* series of novels that have sold fifty million copies and are based on a fundamentalist dispensational theology. More spats will surely arise about whether bare midriffs and rock music are appropriate for worship services and whether women can be ordained.

In short, conservative Christianity in America – and, I believe, in many other parts of the world – is not a phalanx marching in lock step. It is moving, changing – and dividing. Current research indicates that the evangelical and Pentecostal movements in Latin America are not spawning a Latin equivalent of the North American religious right. In Brazil, for example, evangelicals helped elect 'Lula', the candidate of the democratic left Workers' Party, as president. Worldwide, evangelical movements are moving, changing and dividing. They are vigorous in many ways, but often ambivalent about its mission. Many of its leaders, while they once condemned the 'social gospel' are now searching for a social theology of their own that would include peacemaking, striving for racial justice, combating poverty. The opportunity for useful conversation with the 'other wing' (which is also in motion) may be more promising than ever.

Maybe the next sessions of the World's Parliament of Religions, wherever it is held, should devote a larger portion of its energies to *intra-* as well as *inter*faith dialogue.

Our paradox today for advocates and participants in religious peacemaking is this: we live in the best of times and in the worst of times. We need to turn our attention to the religious dimensions of political strife and the political dimensions of religious discord. We need to face in three directions: towards other faiths, towards the 'other wing' in our own tradition and towards the complex political context of the fractured world in which we carry on our work. If we can manage this, we may transform the devil's triangle that often hampers our effectiveness, not into a Christian Trinity or a Hindu Trimurti, but into a humble and sturdy tripod that serves the kind of future we all want.

Glossary

Adams, James Luther (1901–94), famous American theologian; he served as professor at Harvard University and taught at Meadville Lombard Theological School; influential Unitarian minister in the USA.

Analects, also known as the *Analects of Confucius*; it is the records of words, deeds and conversations of Confucius and his disciples; a major classic of Confucianism.

Anti-Vietnam War Movement, along with the Civil Rights Movement, spread in the USA in the 1960s, as the Vietnam War (1960–75) escalated.

Apartheid, Afrikaans word meaning separateness or apartness; meaning the legal system of racial segregation adopted by South Africa from 1948 to 1990 and abolished in 1991.

Baptist Church, one of the largest groups of Protestants; it began in seventeenth-century England, with many believers in the USA. It is the largest denomination among African Americans.

Bhagavad-Gita, important sacred writing for the Vishnu school of Hinduism. It is a part of *Mahābhārata*, the ancient Indian religious and philosophical verses, and takes the form of a conversation between Arjuna and Sri Krishna, who is considered to be the embodiment of Lord himself.

Bodhisattva Never Disparaging, appears in the twentieth chapter of the Lotus Sutra; he deeply respects the people he meets, in spite of their slander against him, because he believes that they have innate potential to become Buddhas.

Boston Research Center for the 21st Century, founded in 1993 in Cambridge, Massachusetts by Daisaku Ikeda; it works to build cultures of peace through dialogue and educational programmes, including public forums, scholarly seminars and publications. It was renamed the Ikeda Center for Peace, Learning, and Dialogue in July 2009.

Boulding, Elise (b. 1920), Norwegian-American sociologist and peace activist; she served as secretary-general of the International Peace Research Association and was the international chair of the Women's International League for Peace and Freedom; she was co-author with Daisaku Ikeda of *Building a Century of a Culture of Peace*.

Buber, Martin (1878–1965), Israeli philosopher and theologian; he worked as a Jewish spiritual leader and was known for his dialectical philosophy; his major work *I and Thou* greatly influenced psychopathology and psychoanalysis.

Buddha nature, the Buddhahood inherent in all living beings; the Lotus Sutra asserts that all people without exception possess the possibility of attaining Buddhahood.

Buddha's Legacy Teaching Sutra, said to have been preached by Shakyamuni Buddha just before his death; this describes the precepts and teachings for his disciples to follow after his death.

Caine, Hall (1853–1931), British author, journalist and best-selling writer of his times, author of *The Eternal City*.

Center for the Study of World Religions (CSWR), established at Cambridge, Massachusetts, in 1960 to research the major religions in the world; it promotes mutual exchange between people with different beliefs.

Chaplain, clergyman dedicated to charity work at chapels of non-church buildings such as schools and hospitals.

Civil Rights Movement, human rights movement carried out in the 1950s and 1960s by African Americans who called for the abolition of unjust discrimination in education, job opportunities and elections; it led to the enforcement of Civil Rights Law.

Confucianism, major Chinese philosophical and ethical teaching that originated from the teachings of Confucius; it influenced other Asian countries such as Japan and Korea.

Confucius Institutes, educational institutions established worldwide to promote Chinese language and culture; 307 Confucius institutes have been built in 78 countries and territories (as of November 2008).

Declaration for the Abolition of Nuclear Weapons, address by Josei Toda, the second president of Soka Gakkai, on 8 September 1957 at Mitsuzawa Stadium in Yokohama.

Economic Warfare, defensive economic policies that reserve critical economic resources for military use, offensive economic policies that deprive perceived enemies of those resources.

Edison, Thomas Alva (1847–1931), American inventor who developed various devices such as telephone, phonograph, incandescent lightbulb, wireless telegraphy and electric railway.

ElBaradei, Mohamed (b. 1942), general director of the International Atomic Energy Agency (IAEA) from 1997; together with IAEA he was awarded the Nobel Peace Prize in 2005. He entered the Egyptian Ministries of External Affairs in 1964.

Emerson, Ralph Waldo (1803–82), American poet and thinker; known as a transcendentalist, greatly influenced American literature and thinkers in the late nineteenth century; author of such works as *Nature, The American Scholar* and *Divinity College Address.*

Foreign Affairs, American journal from the Council on Foreign Relations (CFR), first published in 1922; it deals with international relations and is published six times a year.

Freire, Paulo (1921–97), Brazilian educational theorist and influential promoter of literacy education; he served as the Secretary of Education for São Paulo and was awarded the UNESCO Prize for Peace Education in 1986; he is the author of *Pedagogy of the Oppressed.*

Galbraith, John Kenneth (1908–2006), American economist and professor at Harvard University, president of American Economic Association and the deputy administrator in the Office of Price Administration under President Franklin D. Roosevelt; the co-author with Daisaku Ikeda of *Toward Creating an Age of Humanism.*

Gandhi, Mohandas Karamchand, 'Mahatma Gandhi' (1869–1948), Indian political leader and thinker; committed to civil rights movement in South Africa; he became the leader of the Indian nationalist movement against British rule and was esteemed for his doctrine of non-violent protest and civil disobedience.

Global Citizenship, advocated by Josei Toda, second president of Soka Gakkai; this is an idealistic view of the human race as one family living together on earth, transcending national, racial and cultural boundaries.

Great Depression, the largest depression in world history; said to have been triggered by the stock market crash on 24 October 1929, known as Black Thursday.

Half-day School System, proposed by Tsunesaburo Makiguchi in his *Education for Creative Living*; this idea emphasizes both knowledge gained in classrooms and experiences in real life; it is aimed at nurturing children's personalities by having them spend the half-day at school and the rest of the day doing productive work outside classrooms.

Hard Power, generally refers to physical power such as military power in international relations.

Huntington, Samuel P. (1927–2008), professor of political science at Harvard University; he was a member of the US National Security Council between 1977 and 1978; best known for his book *The Clash of Civilizations*.

Iranian Islamic Revolution, led to the collapse of Mohammad Reza Pahlavi's monarchy in 1979 and established an Islamic republic with Ruhollah Khomeini as supreme leader; the revolution created the constitution of the Islamic Republic of Iran and laid a political foundation based on Islamic ideals.

Jesus Family, independent church founded in 1920s in Shandong, China; active mainly in rural areas.

Ji Xianlin (1911–2009), Chinese historian, writer and linguist, who served as chairman of various institutions such as the Chinese Foreign Literature Association; co-author with Daisaku Ikeda and Jiang Zhongxin of *Dialogue on Oriental Wisdom*.

John Paul II, Pope (1920–2005), elected the Bishop of Rome, the leader of the Roman Catholic Church, in 1978.

Kennedy, Edward Moore (b. 1932), American politician and youngest brother of US President John F. Kennedy; he was Senator for Massachusetts.

Kennedy, John Fitzgerald (1917–63), thirty-fifth president of the USA; he negotiated vigorously with leaders in Communist countries and faced challenges such as the Cuban Missile Crisis, the building of the Berlin Wall and the Vietnam War.

Kennedy, Robert Francis (1925–68), American politician and lawyer, the younger brother of John F. Kennedy; he served as attorney general in Kennedy presidency and ran for presidential nomination opposing the Vietnam War; he was assassinated during the presidential nomination campaign.

Keshin-Mecchi, literally means 'reducing the body to ashes and annihilating consciousness'; a reference to the Hinayana doctrine that asserts nirvana can be attained only upon extinguishing one's body and mind.

Khatami, Seyyed Mohammad (b. 1943), Iranian politician and scholar who served as chairman of Islamic Centre in Hamburg until returning to Iran during the Iranian Revolution in 1979; he was elected president in 1997, and was the first Iranian president to visit the West; he contributed to improving international relations.

King, Martin Luther, Jr. (1929–68), leader of the American Civil Rights Movement; he led the movement using non-violent means and greatly contributed to alleviating discrimination towards black people.

Kissinger, Henry (b. 1923), American politician and political scientist; he was national security adviser under President Nixon and contributed to the restoration of US–China relationships and the conclusion of the Paris Peace Accords that ended the Vietnam War; he was awarded Nobel Peace Prize in 1973 and was co-author with Daisaku Ikeda of *Philosophy of Human Peace*.

Kosygin, Alexei (1904–80), premier of the Soviet Union (1964–80); he mediated between India and Pakistan during the India–Pakistan border war; his talks with then US President Lyndon B. Johnson and Chinese Premier Zhou Enlai helped alleviate international tensions.

League of Nations, established in 1920 as the first international peace organization in history; although over sixty countries joined, it did not function as expected, largely due to America's non-participation.

Liberal Arts, college or university curriculum where students learn primarily general knowledge in the humanities, in contrast to a professional or technical curriculum; the concept originated in medieval Europe.

Liberation Theology, espoused in the Latin American Episcopal Conference (CELAM) meeting in 1968 in Medellín, Columbia; it uses the social sciences, especially Marxism, to help understand economic factors that cause poverty and class struggles.

Lifton, Robert J. (b. 1926), American psychiatrist and psychologist, who served as a professor at Yale University; he was an early proponent of psychohistory and was author of *Death in Life: Survivors of Hiroshima*.

Lotus Sutra, Mahayana Buddhist sutra edited in Sanskrit; the Chinese translation by Kumārajīva has been widely used; it has greatly influenced culture of many countries such as China and Japan.

Makiguchi, Tsunesaburo (1871–1944), Japanese geographer and educator who advocated value-creating pedagogy; he was the founding president of Soka Gakkai; during the Second World War he opposed Japanese military government and Shinto support for it; he was imprisoned in violation of Peace Preservation Law and died in prison.

Mandela, Nelson (b. 1918), former president of South Africa, who carried out non-violent protests against apartheid and was charged with act of treason, convicted, and sentenced to life imprisonment; after twenty-seven years in prison, he was released in 1990 and became the first president of free and democratic South Africa (1994–9).

Manhattan Project, US project during the Second World War to develop and produce nuclear weapons; it was implemented by such scientists as Earnest Lawrence, Leó Szilárd, Enrico Fermi and directed by Robert Oppenheimer and resulted in the production and detonation of atomic bombs at Hiroshima and Nagasaki, Japan, in 1945.

Mays, Benjamin (1894?–1984), first African American to learn from Gandhi, and the sixth president of Morehouse College (1940–67); he influenced spiritual aspects of the civil rights movement and delivered the eulogy to Martin Luther King, Jr. as his life-long mentor.

McNamara, Robert (1916–2009), American businessman, secretary of defense under Presidents John F. Kennedy and Lyndon B. Johnson during the Cuban Missile Crisis and Vietnam War.

Mennonites, Christian Anabaptist denomination named after Menno Simons (1496–1561) and active in the USA; Mennonites are known for their objection to infant baptism, refusal to take public office, and conscientious objection; they do volunteer activities around the world addressing pacifism based on the Bible.

Methodist, Protestant Christian denomination founded by Anglican clergyman John Wesley (1703–91); committed to social reformation and education based on stoic religious lives.

Middle Way, a way of life that avoids extremes, rejecting opposite extremes such as sufferings and joy, self-indulgence and self-mortification, and existence and non-existence; the Middle Way follows Tiantai's interpretation that the true nature of all things exhibits both non-substantiality and temporary existence.

Milinda, also known as Menander I, ruled c. 115–90 BC; conquered Afghanistan and India as a Greek king; he extended his kingdom into the Ganges River basin through the province of Punjab; he embraced Buddhism after a conversation with the Buddhist sage Nāgasena.

Montgomery Bus Boycott, originated from an incident in 1955 in which Rosa Parks was arrested for refusing to give up her seat in a city bus to a white man; as a protest against unfair racial discrimination in the USA the bus boycott started from Montgomery, Alabama, and spread among black people.

Mysticism, refers to religions or forms of religions that value sacred personal experience and seek salvation in direct communication or identity with the divine, ultimate reality or God.

Nāgasena, Indian Buddhist sage (c. 150 BC); his conversation with Greek King Milinda on Buddhism is recorded in *Milinda Panha* and is said to represent the exchange of wisdom between the East and West.

Nietzsche, Friedrich Wilhelm (1844–1900), German philosopher; known for his critique of Christianity and traditional morality; his influence is said to remain within and beyond philosophy in existentialism and postmodernism; he was the author of *Thus Spoke Zarathustra*.

Nixon, Richard (1913–94), thirty-seventh president of the USA; ended military intervention in the Vietnam War; he resigned the presidency in 1974 after political scandals.

Non-Proliferation Treaty (NPT), Treaty on the Non-Proliferation of Nuclear Weapons, signed by sixty-two countries in 1968 and effective from 1970; 189 signatory countries at present time.

Nuclear Arms: Threat to our World Exhibition, held by Soka Gakkai International with the sponsorship of the UN Department of Public Information to show the horrors and devastating effects of nuclear weapons and wars; the first exhibition was held at the United Nations Headquarters in 1982; it has been shown in thirty-nine cities of twenty-four countries.

Oppenheimer, J. Robert (1904–67), American theoretical physicist, first director of the Manhattan Project at the Los Alamos National Laboratory in New Mexico; he has been called the 'father of the atomic bomb'.

Ortega y Gasset, José (1883–1955), Spanish philosopher and existential humanist; he was a writer who contributed to Spain's twentieth-century cultural and literary renaissance; best-known for *The Revolt of the Masses*.

Penicillin, the first antibiotic, discovered by Alexander Fleming in 1928; it is used for the treatment of bacterial diseases such as pneumonia and sepsis.

Penn, William (1644–1718), joined the Quakers while he was studying at Oxford University and was imprisoned several times for fighting against the authoritative power of the church and the king; he was a champion of liberty and human rights in America and founder of the state of Pennsylvania.

Picasso, Pablo (1881–1973), Spanish painter and sculptor, the co-founder of Cubism and member of the Surrealist school; he developed unique painting styles and opened a path to modern painting.

Plato (c. 427–347 BC), ancient Greek philosopher and disciple of Socrates; the author of such works as *The Republic* and *Apology*.

Proposal for the Normalization of Japan–China Relations, delivered by Daisaku Ikeda in September 1968 at the eleventh Student Division General Meeting of Soka Gakkai; it proposed concrete steps to normalize the relationship between Japan and China, such as officially recognizing the government of the People's Republic of China, Chinese membership in the UN and promoting bilateral economic and cultural exchange.

Puritan, Protestant Christian religious group that opposed doctrines and ceremonies of the Church of England in the sixteenth and seventeenth centuries, seeking more purity of worship and doctrine during the English Reformation.

Quakers, members of the Religious Society of Friends, founded by George Fox in the mid-seventeenth century; William Penn contributed to its expansion into the USA; Quakers believe in the inner light within every person, oppose violence and wars and maintain pacifism; the movement is known for conscientious objection to military service.

Rajiv Gandhi Institute for Contemporary Studies, founded by the Rajiv Gandhi Foundation in 1991; it is a research institute that seeks solutions to contemporary problems from political, economic and legal perspectives.

Rauschenbusch, Walter (1861–1918), American minister and leading figure of the Social Gospel movement in the USA; following Christ's life and teachings described in the Gospels, he tackled social problems to improve the conditions of workers and seek the Kingdom of God.

Rotblat, Joseph (1908–2005), Polish-born English physicist who left the Manhattan Project for reasons of conscience; he was one of the signers of the Russell–Einstein Manifesto that called for scientists to tackle the crisis of nuclear wars, and was co-founder of the Pugwash Conferences on Science and World Affairs; awarded the Nobel Peace Prize in 1995 and was co-author with Daisaku Ikeda of *A Quest for Global Peace*.

Russian Orthodox Church, Christian denomination with the largest following in Russia; it belongs to the Eastern Orthodox Church.

St Francis of Assisi (1181?–1226), founder of the Franciscans, or the Order of Friars Minor; following Jesus, he lived with the spirit of charity; he loved the natural world such as birds and flowers, as seen in his poem and prayer 'The Canticle of the Sun'.

Sangha, Sanskrit or Pali, meaning assembly, association or community formed with shared ideals or principles; in ancient India autonomous organizations were called *sangha*; eventually the word came to mean groups of those who practise Buddhism.

Schiller, Friedrich (1759–1805), German poet, dramatist and philosopher who maintained friendship with Goethe; together they opened a golden age of what is now called Weimar Classicism; his main dramas include *The Robbers* and *Don Carlos*.

Semitic, ethnic groups who have traditionally spoken the Semitic languages, including Arabian, Ethiopian and Hebrew; Judaism, Christianity and Islam originated in the Semitic cultural sphere.

Shakyamuni, also known as Gautama Buddha, founder of Buddhism; born in what is now southern Nepal; though the son of Shuddhodana, the king of the Shākyas, he left the royal palace seeking a solution to the sufferings of life – birth, ageing, sickness and death; according to Buddhist tradition he was born in 1029 BC and died 949 BC, but recent studies have him living nearly 500 years later.

Sikhs, originated mainly from the teachings of Guru Nanak Devu (1469–1538); Sikhism is a revolutionary movement in Hinduism, denying absolute faith in Hinduism and Islam, it tries to synthesize both.

Socrates (c. 470–399 BC), ancient Greek philosopher who used the dialectic method to lead people to enlightenment; he was known for his saying: 'I know that I know nothing.'

Soft Power, often used in contrast to hard power; the phrase generally refers to influence based on knowledge, information and culture and thoughts in international relations.

Song Jian (b. 1931), Chinese scientist and technology policy maker; he was president of the China–Japan Friendship Association and an expert in cybernetics; he was the Chinese representative at the Earth Summit of 1992.

Southern Christian Leadership Conference (SCLC), founded in 1957 in New Orleans by founder-president Martin Luther King, Jr.; a hundred ministers from ten southern states participated, supporting the civil rights movement through non-violent means.

Soyinka, Wole (b. 1934), Nigerian poet and playwright, a contributor to Nigerian politics during the civil war and imprisoned for twenty-two months; he was the author of *The Lion* *and the Jewel* and *A Dance in the Forest*; the first African awarded the Nobel Prize in Literature.

Spanish Civil War (1936–39), rebellion fomented in Spain after the attempted coup d'état by Francisco Franco in 1936; the war devastated Spain, and Franco's Nationalist troops overthrew the Republic government.

Structural Violence, concept used by Johan Galtung, Norwegian peace researcher, to describe poverty and oppression in developing countries resulting not only from internal causes but also from international and domestic social and economic systems.

Swaminathan, Monkombu (b. 1925), Indian agricultural scientist and past president of the Pugwash Conferences on Science and World Affairs; he was co-author with Daisaku Ikeda of *Revolutions: To Green the Environment, to Grow the Human Heart*.

Tehranian, Majid (b. 1937), professor emeritus of the University of Hawaii; first director of the Toda Institute for Global Peace and Policy Research (1996–2008); he specializes in international communications, political science and the study of the Middle East; he is co-author with Daisaku Ikeda of *Global Civilization: A Buddhist–Islamic Dialogue*.

Tillich, Paul (1886–1965), German religious philosopher persecuted by Nazis in Germany, exiled to the USA; he served as professor at Harvard University and developed creative thoughts on religion and culture; best known for *The Courage to Be*.

Toda, Josei (1900–58), disciple of Tsunesaburo Makiguchi and second president of Soka Gakkai; during the Second World War he opposed the Japanese military government and was imprisoned with Makiguchi; he laid the foundation for Soka

Gakkai's development and established philosophical background and guidelines for its peace movement.

Toda Institute for Global Peace and Policy Research, founded in 1996 based on second president of Soka Gakkai Josei Toda's peace philosophy; it has offices in Tokyo and Honolulu and sponsors research programmes on global peace and human security policy issues.

Tönnies, Ferdinand (1855–1936), German sociologist whose ideas, especially those expressed in *Gemeinschaft and Gesellschaft*, greatly influenced sociological theory; he was engaged vigorously in the study of statistics, public opinion and methodology.

Toynbee, Arnold Joseph (1889–1975), English historian who developed a unique view of history that focuses on the cycle of rise, flowering and decline of civilizations; he was the author of *A Study of History* and co-author with Daisaku Ikeda of *Choose Life: A Dialogue*.

Truth and Reconciliation Commission, assembled in 1994 to investigate the human rights violations and political suppression under apartheid in South Africa.

Tu Weiming (b. 1940), American scholar specializing in Confucianism, professor of Chinese history and philosophy at Harvard University; he participated in the UN Eminent Persons' Group meeting held in 2001 representing Confucian civilization and was co-author with Daisaku Ikeda of *A Global Conscience: Dialogue instead of Clash*.

Unity of Heaven and Humanity, a Chinese concept that perceives heaven and humanity not as contradictory but as inherently harmonious and tries to restore the unity; it is a central thought in Chinese philosophy such as Taoism and Confucianism.

Untouchable, people of the lowest social status in India, considered the most unclean in the discriminatory caste system in India.

Weber, Max (1864–1920), German sociologist who contributed to the rationalization in sociology of organizational theory; he is known for his study of sociology of religion; author of such works as *The Protestant Ethic and the Spirit of Capitalism*.

Wilson, Thomas Woodrow (1856–1924), twenty-eighth President of the USA; he proposed what is known as the Fourteen Points that advocated the founding of the League of Nations and called for national self-determination; he was awarded the Nobel Peace Prize in 1919.

Wyeth-Ayerst Laboratories, also known as Wyeth Pharmaceuticals; founded by John and Frank Wyeth in 1860 in Philadelphia, now selling products in over 145 countries.

Yalman, Nur (b. 1931), leading Turkish social anthropologist and professor at Harvard University who carried out fieldwork in many countries; he is known for his study of relations of religion and society and was co-author with Daisaku Ikeda of *A Passage to Peace: Global Solutions from East and West*.

Youth Air Corps, air corps of Imperial Japanese Army formed by young volunteers in the Second World War.

Zhou Enlai (1898–1976), first premier of China (1949–76), known for contributions to the normalization of Sino-Japanese relationships and the conclusion of the Sino-Soviet Treaty of Friendship; he exercised leadership in domestic administration and foreign affairs at the founding of the People's Republic of China.

Notes

Chapter 3

1 Ferdinand Tönnies, *Community and Society* (Dover Publications, New York, 2002).
2 Arnold Toynbee and Daisaku Ikeda, *Choose Life* (Oxford University Press, New York, 1989), p. 335.
3 Nichiren, *The Record of the Orally Transmitted Teachings*, translated by Burton Watson (Soka Gakkai, Tokyo, 2004), p. 146.

Chapter 4

1 Pope John Paul II, 'Internet: A New Forum for Proclaiming the Gospel', 12 May 2002.
2 Nichiren, *The Writings of Nichiren Daishonin* (Soka Gakkai, Tokyo, 1999), p. 286.
3 Harvey Cox, *Turning East* (Simon & Schuster, New York, 1977).
4 Martin Luther King, Jr., *The Autobiography of Martin Luther King, Jr.*, edited by Clayborne Carson (Abacus, London, 1999), p. 19.
5 Cox, *Turning East*.

Chapter 5

1 Harvey Cox, in Douglas Johnston and Cynthia Sampson (eds), *Religion, the Missing Dimension of Statecraft* (Oxford University Press, New York, 1994), ch. 12, p. 272.

Chapter 6

1 Joseph Rotblat and Daisaku Ikeda, *A Quest for Global Peace* (I.B.Tauris, London, 2007), p. 49.
2 *The Lotus Sutra*, translated by Burton Watson (Columbia University Press, New York, 1993), p. 266.

Chapter 7

1 *Questions of King Milinda* (Buddhism in Translations), translated by Henry Clark Warren (Motilal Banarsidass, Delhi, 1998), p. 128.

Chapter 8

1 Rotblat and Ikeda, *A Quest for Global Peace*, p. 90.
2 Plato, *Euthyphro, Apology, Crito*, translated by Benjamin Jowett (Agora Publications, Millis, MA, 2005), p. 44.
3 Plato, *The Last Days of Socrates: Euthyphro, Apology, Crito, Phaedo* (Penguin Classics, London, 1954), p. 86.

Appendix 1

1 Nichiren, *The Writings of Nichiren Daishonin*, vol. 2 (Soka Gakkai, Tokyo, 2006), p. 759
2 J. Takakusu, ed., *Taisho Issaikyo* (Taisho Issaikyo Publishing Society, Tokyo, 1925), vol. 9, p. 43c.
3 Nichiren, *The Record of the Orally Transmitted Teachings*, p. 212.
4 J. Takakusu, ed., *Nanden Daizokyo* (Taisho Shinshu Daizokyo Publishing Society, Tokyo, 1935), vol. 7, pp. 27ff.
5 Takakusu, ed., *Nanden Daizokyo*, vol. 24, p. 358.
6 Josiah Royce, *The Basic Writings of Josiah Royce* (University of Chicago Press, Chicago, 1969), vol. 2, p. 1122.
7 Takakusu, ed., *Nanden Daizokyo*, vol. 11a, p. 137.
8 Nichiren, *The Writings of Nichiren Daishonin*, p. 765.
9 Takakusu, ed., *Taisho Issaikyo*, vol. 30.
10 Nichiren, *The Writings of Nichiren Daishonin*, p. 280.
11 Nichiren, *The Writings of Nichiren Daishonin*, vol. 2, p. 62.
12 John Dewey, *A Common Faith* (Yale University Press, New Haven, CT, 1934), pp. 50–2.
13 Nichiren, *The Record of the Orally Transmitted Teachings*, p. 214.
14 Johann Wolfgang von Goethe, *Faust: A Tragedy*, translated by Bayard Taylor (Modern Library, New York, 1967), pp. 17–18.

15 Johann Wolfgang von Goethe, *Conversations of Goethe with Johann Peter Eckermann* (J.M. Dent and Sons, London, 1930), p. 101.

16 Takakusu, ed., *Nanden Daizokyo*, vol. 13, pp. 1ff.

17 Takakusu, ed., *Nanden Daizokyo*, vol. 23, p. 42.

18 Takakusu, ed., *Taisho Issaikyo*, vol. 1, pp. 645c, 15b.

19 Ralph Waldo Emerson, *Essays and Poems of Emerson* (Harcourt, Brace and Co., New York, 1921), p. 45.

20 Walt Whitman, *Leaves of Grass* (Doubleday & Co., Garden City, NJ, 1926), p. 348.

21 Nichiren, *The Record of the Orally Transmitted Teachings*, p. 90.

Further Reading

Bird, Kai, and Martin J. Sherwin, *American Prometheus: The Triumph and Tragedy of J. Robert Oppenheimer* (Atlantic Books, New York, 2009).

Caine, Hall, *The Eternal City* (Heinemann, London, 1901).

Cox, Harvey, *Turning East* (Simon & Schuster, New York, 1977).

Cox, Harvey, *Religion in the Secular City: Toward a Postmodern Theology* (Simon & Schuster, New York, 1984).

Cox, Harvey, *The Future of Faith* (HarperOne, New York, 2009).

Cox, Harvey, *The Secular City: Secularization and Urbanization in Theological Perspective* (SCM Press, London, 1965).

Dewey, John, *A Common Faith* (Yale University Press, New Haven, CT, 1934).

Emerson, Ralph Waldo, *Essays and Poems of Emerson* (Harcourt, Brace and Co., New York, 1921).

Freire, Paulo, *Pedagogy of the Oppressed* (Continuum, London, 1970).

Goethe, Johann Wolfgang von, *Conversations of Goethe with Johann Peter Eckermann* (J.M. Dent and Sons, London, 1930).

Goethe, Johann Wolfgang von, *Faust: A Tragedy*, translated by Bayard Taylor (Modern Library, New York, 1967).

Huntington, Samuel P., 'The Clash of Civilizations', *Foreign Affairs*, vol. 72, no. 43 (1993).

Ikeda, Daisaku, *The Human Revolution*, 6 vols (Weatherhill Inc, New York, 1973–2000).

Johnston, Douglas and Cynthia Sampson, eds, *Religion, the Missing Dimension of Statecraft* (Oxford University Press, New York, 1994).

King, Martin Luther, Jr., *The Autobiography of Martin Luther King, Jr.*, edited by Clayborne Carson (Abacus, London, 1999).

The Lotus Sutra, translated by Burton Watson (Columbia University Press, New York, 1993).

Nichiren, *The Record of the Orally Transmitted Teachings*, translated by Burton Watson (Soka Gakkai, Tokyo, 2004).

Nichiren, *The Writings of Nichiren Daishonin* (Soka Gakkai, Tokyo, 1999 and 2006).

Ortega y Gasset, José, *Mission of the University* (Transaction Publishers, New Brunswick, NJ, 1992).

Plato, *The Republic* (Oxford Classics, Oxford, 2007).

Plato, *Euthyphro, Apology, Crito*, translated by Benjamin Jowett (Agora Publications, Millis, MA, 2005).

Plato, *The Last Days of Socrates: Euthyphro, Apology, Crito, Phaedo* (Penguin Classics, London, 1954).

Questions of King Milinda (Buddhism in Translations), translated by Henry Clark Warren (Motilal Banarsidass, Delhi, 1998).

Rotblat, Joseph, 'Leaving the Bomb Project', *Bulletin of the Atomic Scientists* (August 1985) pp. 16–18.

Rotblat, Joseph, and Daisaku Ikeda, *A Quest for Global Peace* (I.B.Tauris, London, 2007).

Royce, Josiah, *The Basic Writings of Josiah Royce* (University of Chicago Press, Chicago, 1969).

Takakusu, J., ed., *Taisho Issaikyo* (Taisho Issaikyo Publishing Society, Tokyo, 1925).

Takakusu, J., ed., *Nanden Daizokyo* (Taisho Shinshu Daizokyo Publishing Society, Tokyo, 1935).

Tönnies, Ferdinand, *Community and Society* (Dover Publications, New York, 2002).

Toynbee, Arnold, and Daisaku Ikeda, *Choose Life: A Dialogue* (Oxford University Press, Oxford, 1989).

Weber, Max, *Politics as a Vocation* (Fortress Press, Minneapolis, 1965).

Whitman, Walt, *Leaves of Grass* (Doubleday & Co., Garden City, NJ, 1926).

Index